THE COLLECTABLE WORLD OF

MABEL LUCIE ATTWELL

Watercolour by Mabel Lucie Attwell. An imaginative self-portrait of the artist with her daughter, Peggy, 1909.

THE COLLECTABLE WORLD OF

Mabel Lucie Attwell

BY

JOHN HENTY

RICHARD DENNIS
1999

ACKNOWLEDGEMENTS

For me, this book represents a long journey of discovery and, with its publication, I feel all fellow travellers on the Attwell highway deserve very special thanks. Together we made it!

To Ralph and Ineke Gockel for their unfailing support and encouragement over a number of years. To Richard Dennis, my publisher and his staff, Wendy Wort and Sue Evans. To the team at Flaydemouse in Yeovil. To Patricia and Ian Aspinall, Norman and Marjorie Attwell, Chris Beetles, Beryl Delve, Anne and Leonara Excell of Bookmark, the people of Fowey, Cornwall, where much of this book was written, Eunice Fox, Wallace Grevatt, Nick Hayley, Adam Lovejoy, the late Henry Morgan, Barbara Richardson, Jennifer Rose, Vivienne Truran for access to her wonderful collection, Pat and Alan Walters, David and Paula Whitfield, John and Hilary Wickham and Mark Wickham. Finally, to my family, Andrew and Marysia and, in particular, my wife Sylvia, for accepting so generously the 'other woman' in my life, and helping me in many ways to chronicle a remarkable career.

THE AUTHOR

John Henty is a broadcaster and has been collecting Mabel Lucie Attwell memorabilia for thirty years. He first became interested in the artist's work when a listener to his programme on BBC Radio Brighton sent in a record request on a Mabel Lucie postcard. Subsequently, in 1977, his interview with Peggy Wickham, the artist's daughter, was broadcast on BBC's *Woman's Hour*. During the early 1970s John Henty also presented *Night Ride* on BBC Radio Two. He is an associate member of the British Guild of Travel Writers and lives with his wife Sylvia, in Lewes in Sussex. In 1996, John and Sylvia opened a Mabel Lucie Attwell museum and shop at 34 Fore Street in Fowey, the Cornish town in which the artist spent her final years. If you are a Mabel Lucie Attwell enthusiast or keen to communicate with other collectors, a regular newsletter is planned. For details of this and other Mabel-related matters, please contact the author at PO Box 900, Lewes, East Sussex, BN7 ITF.

Edited by Sue Evans

Colour photography by Magnus Dennis

Production by Wendy Wort

Print, design and reproduction by Flaydemouse, Yeovil, Somerset

Published by Richard Dennis, The Old Chapel, Shepton Beauchamp, Somerset TA19 0LE, England

© 1999 Lucie Attwell Ltd., Richard Dennis & John Henty

ISBN 0 903685 70 1

All rights reserved

British Library Cataloguing-in-Publication Data. A catalogue record for this book is available from the British Library

Front cover: very rare, whimsical, jointed-cardboard fairy designed for the nursery, Valentine of Dundee, 1920s.

Back cover: from the First World War, Mabel Lucie Attwell prints were produced for framing purposes. Many of those used were of existing postcard designs, others were from book illustrations and some enterprising printers even included an artistic frame and printed caption. Prints from publications such as *The Tatler*, *The Bystander* and *The Illustrated London News* were also framed.

CONTENTS

FOREWORD

Mabel Lucie Attwell was very much a part of my childhood, alongside books such as *Milly Molly Mandy, Swallows and Amazons* and *The Famous Five*. In our more critical age, lashings of ginger beer, party frocks and bows have given way to grunge. So is the work of Mabel Lucie Attwell dated? No, No, No! Many of us long for a kinder, more reflective, less judgemental lifestyle, with more time to allow some sunshine into our lives. Critics could say 'yes' but even in the old days the Terrible Twos weren't always rounded and sweet, or puppies plump and well-behaved, bath tubs steaming, and babies born to loving mummies. Mabel Lucie Attwell's illustrations and sayings 'accentuate the positive' as Johnnie Mercer's song goes – she was an artist with her own style and a cracking imagination and we would be wrong to assume that she had an easy life and this filtered through into her art. It was the very opposite. As the daughter of an East End butcher she really had to struggle to become an accepted artist. Most women work nowadays but this was a rarity in the twenties and thirties, when Mabel was the breadwinner. Rarer still she kept the family together through her work. Her fans fell in love with *Diddums* the doll and followed the adventures of the *Boo-Boos*. She was an entrepreneur and made the most of her creations. They featured on potties, postcards, jigsaws, annuals and plaques. Mabel Lucie was prolific – a life without rose-coloured glasses spurred her on. She was tough, determined and focused. Life was unkind to her; her artist husband lost an arm in the First World War. Brian, her youngest son, died at an early age and, as a widow, she worked on in blitzed London during World War Two. However, she enjoyed peace at the end of her life. For twenty years she lived in a house overlooking the harbour at Fowey. A suitable reward for all the pleasure she has given. Author and broadcaster, John Henty, discovered Mabel Lucie Attwell through his radio show on B.B.C. Radio Brighton. In his own words when he kindly asked me to write this foreword, 'Some requests arrived on Mabel Lucie Attwell postcards, and I was hooked!'

I was on Bruges railway station queuing for the EuroStar back to London the other day. I saw a woman's skirt move in the next queue. What was it? Peeping out at me was a Mabel Lucie Attwell babe. Chubby cheeked, red curls with a blue ribbon, little red skirt, white socks and, yes, big red shoes with bows. We exchanged beams. Need I write more? Mabel Lucie Attwell's tradition is alive and well.

Sarah Kennedy, 1999

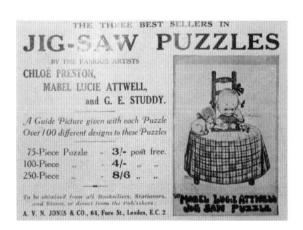

MABEL LUCIE ATTWELL

1879-1964

Mile End Road, East London, birthplace of Mabel Lucie Attwell, c1880.

To a young, sensitive girl the East End of London in the 1880s must have been, at times, an alarming place in which to grow up. With its close proximity to the River Thames and thriving dockland area, thick pea-soup fog was a common occurrence and street violence an everyday reality. This was the London of lamplighter men, horse-drawn buses, costers pushing barrows and devastating poverty. It was the London into which Mabel Lucy Attwell (Lucy became Lucie at an early stage in her artistic career) was born on the 4th June 1879, the sixth of eleven children – four of whom did not survive infancy. And it was the London which contrasted so dramatically with the peace and tranquillity of her final home on the south coast of Cornwall at Fowey where she died on the 5th November 1964, after what she described to her daughter as a 'lively life'.

Lively indeed, and full of contrasts. The happiness of marriage to a fellow artist, Harold Cecil Earnshaw; yet the sadness of his early death at the age of fifty-one. The joy of having three children; only for one of them to die when just twenty years old. The gay and successful years of the Twenties – visiting royalty in Romania and arranging a daughter's wedding. Then the difficult Thirties with an ailing husband and the early divorce of her only daughter, Peggy. Ironically it was these ups and downs in her own life that enabled the artist to relate so accurately to other people's trials and tribulations. Her postcard work in particular was, for almost fifty years, always alert to the delights and the difficulties of everyday life. There is no doubt that this sensitivity to the needs of ordinary people contributed to her great success in all fields of publishing.

Even at a very early age, she was remembered as a shy, sensitive child and was sometimes unkindly called 'the tragedy queen' by her family. She lived in a large redbrick house called Collingwood in Harlesden, north London. Her mother, a very pretty woman named Emily Ann, came from Westbury in Gloucestershire and married the eccentric Augustus Attwell on the 11th February 1869. With a fine, pink, bald head and impressive white moustache Augustus had progressive ideas – he was pro-Boer and keen on homeopathic medicines, it is said that he had seawater brought to his London home for bathing purposes. Somewhat incongruously he was, by profession, a family butcher – the Attwells owned a group of shops in the East End of London, headed by Mabél Lucie's grandfather, Augustus Valentine Attwell, and his brother,

Emily and Augustus Attwell, 1869.

Births page from the family bible.

The under-mentioned Houses are situate within the Boundaries of the							

Census showing the residents of 182 Mile End Road, Mabel Lucie's home, 1881.

Romeo. Later, when providing details for *Who's Who*, Mabel seemed reluctant to reveal that her father was a butcher. Whatever her reasons for this, in the last years of the nineteenth century the business at 182 Mile End Road was very successful, and enabled Mr and Mrs Attwell to provide the best education for their growing family. Mabel attended the Coopers' Company Coborn School just off the Bow Road. Founded in 1536, Coopers' provided a relatively enlightened education for both boys and girls. At the turn of the century, the music hall comediennes, Elsie and Doris Waters, were pupils there, and their younger brother, Jack, (later known as actor, Jack Warner, of *Dixon of Dock Green* fame) attended the boys' school in nearby Tredegar Square. Interestingly, in 1889, Miss Gause, the drawing teacher at Coopers', decided to marry and, under normal circumstances, would have been required to resign. However she was allowed to continue teaching though she had to use her maiden name – presumably this was noted by Mabel Lucie and her fellow scholars.

Sadly, several of the Attwell children died very young. Mabel Lucie's surviving siblings were: Emily Annabella, 24th February 1870; Annie Florence, 11th April 1873; Augustus, 5th September 1874; Ernest George 16th February 1877; Jessie, 21st June 1881; and Norman, 8th May 1888.

Emily, the eldest child, was named after their mother. She attended art school, married fellow illustrator, Tom Overnell, and became a fine watercolourist. Mabel's favourite sister was Annie, six years her senior – apparently they looked very much alike and got on well together in the busy home environment. Annie married and had two children before her death in 1917, while in her early forties. It appears that Jessie was the favoured

child who, according to Mabel Lucie was 'spoilt, malicious and unpleasant'. She was nicknamed 'gig lamps', probably because of the glasses she wore. Jessie became a concert pianist and teamed up with the youngest child, Norman, (who married an actress whose stage name was Amé Stewart) and who, during a long career as a principal cellist, was associated with several major orchestras including the Bournemouth Symphony and Royal Philharmonic. Not surprisingly, Collingwood was full of music and music-making with Jessie and Norman rehearsing the family orchestra which also drew on friends who played other instruments. Mabel Lucie recalled in *Modern Woman*, October 1961:

Jessie and Norman, Mabel Lucie's sister and brother.

Gus and Ernest, Mabel Lucie's brothers, on the stage.

Norman's wife, the actress, Amé Stewart.

'When anyone visited our home there would be one of the children practising a different musical instrument. I played the piano – or at least tried to. My mother used to sigh, "oh! please, not now Mab", as soon as I opened the lid of the piano. My father, who was a perfectionist, would say patiently, "It isn't right Mab", and you know I inherited that streak of perfectionism. Sometimes I've been forced to end a contract because I must have my pictures perfect.'

Although Collingwood had its cosy side with coal fires, the cooking of large batches of pastry, cakes and joints on the shining black kitchen range, life there and in the Mile End Road was far from perfect for Mabel Lucie Attwell. She told her daughter Peggy of being afraid of a tiger in the cupboard at the turn of the stairs; that she had chilblains

Left, Augustus, right, Emily, centre their son, Norman, with his son, Norman, who became a professional artist, c1927.

on her hands every winter and that water in the bedroom jug would be frozen in the morning. She suffered agonies from toothache because her father, who favoured sizeable slabs of toffee, did not approve of dentists. She remembered a woman visitor asking her mother, 'What is it about that child – there is something behind her eyes', which sent Mabel Lucie rushing to the mirror to search for whatever this 'something' might be. She had rheumatic fever as a girl and believed that this changed her into a tall, long-faced person. Nervous of strange men, she would quake if she thought a man was looking at her in the street. Mabel Lucie craved family affection and remembered praying in the lavatory for her mother to like her. She also desperately wanted a doll and was, at one stage, 'besotted' with babies in prams. Sadly, on one occasion at least, her birthday was completely forgotten.

These were the times when she would take refuge in her own vivid imagination and scribble in notebooks and make secret sketches. Encouraged by her older sister, Emily, she began to write stories and illustrate them – even exercise books were covered with sketches and images of other children. She was adept at creating a suitably witty caption to her drawings which, later, proved to be a valuable asset.

There are differing versions of how Mabel Lucie first came to be paid for her sketches and drawings. The artist herself said in an interview in 1955 with Elizabeth Hickson of the *Daily Express*:

'When I was fifteen, my family thought I'd gone completely mad. While they were becoming brilliant musicians, I suddenly announced that I'd taken two pictures to a publisher. I can even remember what I wore on that fateful day. A grey, jersey dress with black ribbed stockings and my long brown hair tied back under a hat with daisies on the brim. I simply wanted to earn some pocket money, as I never seemed to have any in the ordinary way – my brothers always borrowed it. They jeered and said I was making a silly fool of myself. However, a few days later, I received an envelope by post. They were all watching me and when I opened it – inside was a cheque for two guineas.'

Clearly the brothers were impressed, but it appears her father decided to take her modest earnings as a matter of course and still required her to 'attend to the cooking' at home. Not for much longer though. That initial success was all that the determined teenager needed to find more work and enrol at a private art school, Heatherley's, the oldest of its kind in London, and then at St. Martin's School of Art. Mabel Lucie commented in an article by Austin Moore in the mid-1930s:

'Soon after I was doing quite a lot of work for publishers. Not important but it was enough to live on and to pay my fees at the art schools where I studied for five hard years. So you see, practically from the time I finished schooling I was able to earn my bread and butter as an artist.'

Little is known of this early published work. There has been reference to some child studies for *The Tatler*, simple line-drawings appeared in the occasional theatre programme, *Mrs Wiggs of the Cabbage Patch*, a comedy in three acts, and colour-posters were produced for Our Dumb Friends' League in London over a period of years. With these posters there were also accompanying black-and-white postcards used for promotional purposes. These are regarded by many as the artist's very first cards, albeit non-commercial ones. However, without an agent she, like most of her contemporaries, had to seek commissions herself, either by making personal visits to publishing houses or sending sketch samples with a covering letter. In October 1902, she sent eight simple pen-and-ink drawings to Raphael Tuck & Sons Ltd., Fine Art and Book Publishers. The managing director of this prestigious company addressed his reply to M.L. Attwell Esq:

'Dear Sir,

In response to your note with drawings, these are undoubtedly clever but not quite suited to our purposes, with the exception perhaps of the one design You Go Home. You have not stated your price for this. We shall be glad to hear from you on the subject, and perhaps to see a little companion to it.

Yours faithfully etc.'

The reply from M.L. Attwell was prompt. Mabel Lucie decided that if Messrs Tuck & Son were comfortable with offering commissions to a gentleman, then a gentleman she would remain – at least for the time being. It is not clear, however, whether she entered into this subtle subterfuge deliberately or by accident. Neither is it known when Raphael Tuck & Sons were told of the sex-change! On 10th November 1902 the managing director wrote:

'Dear Sir,

We have the companion to the picture selected and have pleasure in enclosing a cheque for one guinea in payment of the two designs. We shall be glad to see further work from time to time. We may say at once that we do not know what use to put these designs to at the present

moment and possibly we may approach you later on with a view to completing a series.'

M.L. Attwell needed no further encouragement and soon more sketches were winging their way from Mile End Road to Raphael House in the city of London. Raphael Tuck & Son were enthusiastic and prepared to give this creative fellow a further trial. However, in a letter dated 15th April 1903, they did add a cautionary note:

'We do not care about the feet of any of your children, which look as if the wearers had clogs on, while there is nothing in the appearance of the children to indicate that they are Dutch. We should like you to look over the designs from this point of view and see what can be done. Yours etc.'

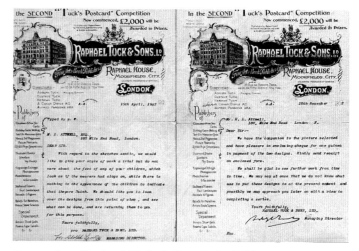

Letters from Raphael Tuck & Sons Ltd., 1902.

Once the 'clogs' were eliminated, or at least modified, and Raphael Tuck came to terms with having a woman artist on their books, the relationship developed into a strong and vital one. As the writer Barbara Richardson wrote in *The Book and Magazine Collector*, July 1993, the *Raphael House Library of Gift Books* was made up of thirty-one volumes, all edited by Captain Edric Vredenburg. These featured pictorial boards with cloth back, or in cloth bevelled, with gilt edges, and each volume came in a box decorated with an identical illustration to the one on the book cover. Of these thirty-one volumes, Mabel Lucie Attwell illustrated six: *Mother Goose*, 1910; *Alice in Wonderland*, 1911; *Grimm's Fairy Tales*, 1912; *Hans Andersen's Fairy Tales*, 1914; *The Water Babies*, 1915; and *Children's Stories from French Fairy Tales*, 1917. 'It is worth noting,' Barbara Richardson adds, 'that another book in the series, *Children's Stories from Scott*, was illustrated by Harold Earnshaw, her husband.'

Mabel Lucie met Harold at St. Martin's School of Art – she was in her late twenties, and he had just celebrated his twentieth birthday. By all accounts, 'Pat', as she called him, was a light-hearted, sociable fellow who had once been a choir boy and retained the appearance of one. He was born in 1886, in Woodford, Essex. His grandfather, Samuel

Harold Earnshaw and Mabel Lucie following their marriage.

her brothers, she noticed his hat on a chair in the hall and kissed it – quickly!), Mabel Lucie had no doubts whatsoever about her love for this cheery, optimistic fellow-student. She told all her friends that he was the man she would marry. And so she did, on her twenty-ninth birthday, the 4th June 1908, but not, it would seem by their absence, with parental approval. An omnibus took the young couple to the Hendon Registry Office and they were married in the presence of Pat's sister, Kitty, and Mabel's brother, Norman. Outside, a street organ serenaded the young couple's departure with the tune, 'When we are married'.

At the time of their marriage, Mabel Lucie had commissions for half-tone illustrations and cover designs for the Edinburgh-based firm of publishers W.&R. Chambers; ten plates for the publication *A Boy and a Secret* by Raymond Jacberns was released later that year. Pat was working mainly for the publishers, Blackie, but may also have had a commission from Chambers. Their honeymoon was spent in Rose Cottage, a picturesque, thatched cottage at Babbacombe Bay in Devon, which was then an unspoilt beauty spot. As she told *Vogue* magazine in 1962:

'We found we had £50 each and that seemed a great deal of money, and quite enough to get married on. So we did and took a cottage in Devon for the summer. He had his book to do and I had mine. We weren't married long but we were happy.'

For the first few months of their new life together, they lived in Wickham Mansions, a modest flat south of the Thames at Dulwich, where the illustrative work flourished and the commissions increased. In that first year, Pat also joined the London Sketch Club which was an opportunity for him to mix with other artists and illustrators on a weekly basis. Situated in Wells Street near Oxford Street, the club was easily reached from suburban Dulwich and provided a hot supper for members. Inevitably, at that time, it was a 'Men Only' establishment. Among the

Earnshaw, was Rector of Sheffield University. Pat's father, Frederick, left Yorkshire and joined a firm of scientific and mathematical instrument-makers in the south. By 1908, he was described as 'being of independent means'. Despite her admitted shyness of the opposite sex (she described one occasion at Collingwood when, silently adoring a friend of

Harold and Mabel Lucie's marriage certificate.

distinguished membership were Charles and William Heath Robinson, Cecil Aldin, Tom Browne, Harry Rountree (a good friend of Pat's with whom he played golf regularly) and G.S. Studdy who was to become famous for his *Bonzo* dog character.

Meanwhile, as Christmas 1908 approached, Mabel Lucie realised with great joy and some apprehension that she was pregnant. Many years later in 1961, when asked by Carolyn Scott of *Modern Woman* what she considered to be her greatest achievement, she hesitated before replying:

'My marriage – no, my first baby. Achievement is the wrong word, but yes, motherhood was the most wonderful thing in my life. My career is me, and my pictures are me, but no artist or writer or scientist, could make anything as perfect as a baby, and yet through me, it had been done. I couldn't believe it.'

The birth was not straightforward. It was a lengthy delivery and not helped, one imagines, by the woman doctor exclaiming on her arrival, 'Oh good, my first patient.'

Marjorie Joan Earnshaw was born on the 13th May 1909. For reasons that have never been fully explained, Marjorie became plain 'Peggy'. Two years later Max Earnshaw was born, only to be renamed 'Peter' or 'Pete'. Probably, the reason for this was that, with the outbreak of the First World War, German-sounding names were disapproved of in England, and often discreetly dropped. The second son, Brian, arrived in 1914 and spent most of his short life being called 'Bill'. With Harold Earnshaw answering to Pat, and Mabel Lucy now signing her work Mabel Lucie, it is little wonder that the biographer may become confused!

With the arrival of their first child, a decision was made to go house-hunting and, using the excellent steam train service that ran throughout suburban south London, Pat and Mabel Lucie found themselves at Coulsdon South railway station, close to the Farthing Downs. After a short walk, they came upon a tiny detached cottage-style house called 'Casita' in Downs Road. They liked the property immediately and welcomed its close proximity to open farmland, the downs and a nine-hole golf course. Today, Downs Road has changed very little though the cottage has gone. This was the first of many house moves, and there was just enough room in the 'little house' for Pat, Mabel, baby Peggy and Nanny Simpson. However, a year later, in the spring of 1911, Peter was born and a move to a larger house nearby became necessary. 'Fairdene', in Fairdene Road, Coulsdon, was a gabled suburban house with a sizeable garden and open land to the north and east. Two upper rooms were joined together to make one large studio where both artists worked; Mabel Lucie illustrating the *Raphael Tuck Gift Books* and Pat completing work on yet another *Blackie Book for Boys*. He was also able to help her from time to time – and was responsible for some of the less 'Attwellish' parts of her pictures, such as real dogs as opposed to *Mops*, the omnipresent pup in so many cards.

Around 1917, the writer, A.B. Cooper visited the Earnshaws at Fairdene, the 'house on the hill' as he called

Advertisement for Valentine and Sons, *The Illustrated London News*, c1918.

it, and, in an article entitled *Harold Earnshaw and his 'right hand'*, described being met in the garden by Peggy and Pete who told him that their parents were upstairs. He found the couple:

'...under 'the top light' with a whole table between them, working for the bread that perisheth and the fame that endureth – and getting both – Mabel Lucie Attwell at a poster which presently will be hung 'on the line' in the free picture gallery of every city in the Empire; the hoarding, and Harold Earnshaw at a toy book which he has promised a firm of publishers to finish in record time.'

The cosy togetherness which is conjured up by this picture is a little misleading for in 1961, Mabel Lucie, with a twinkle in her eyes, was obliged to concede to the journalist, Carolyn Scott:

'...at first when we were married, we tried to do our separate work with our easels just as close as possible. Well, believe me that didn't work. Then we tried easels in different rooms. In the end, we simply had to take studios in different houses!'

By this time, Mabel Lucie had acquired the services of an artists' agent. Francis and Mills claimed to be, with some justification, 'Agents to the Best Artists', and this immodest message was emblazoned across their label which depicted a mediaeval nobleman in a tall-crowned hat, drawn by Sketch Club Member, John Hassall. Alan Francis, a larger-than-life character, full of bustle and good business sense, told an extremely nervous Mabel Lucie at their first meeting in 1910, that he was not interested in

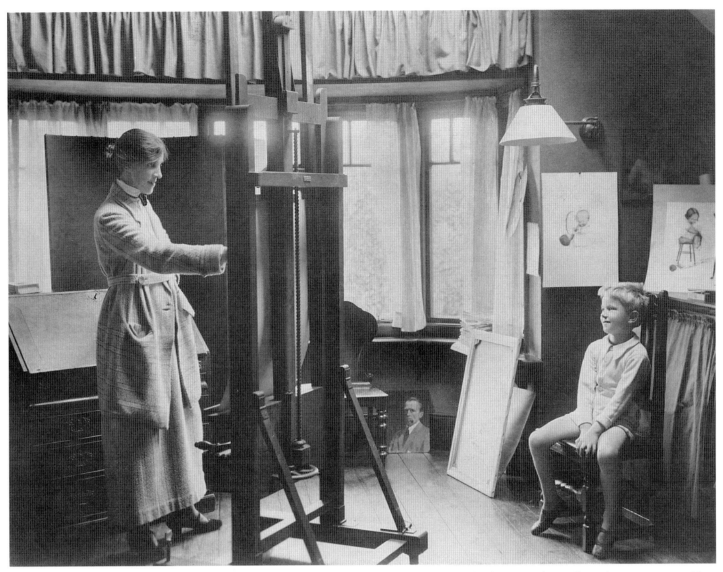

Mabel Lucie at work in her Coulsdon, Surrey home with her youngest son, Brian. The large easel is still in the possession of her grandson, Mark Wickham. This photograph was first published in *The Tatler*, December 1920.

the work of 'young ladies'. However, he did invite her to leave a portfolio of sketches for him to look through, although he made no promises. When she returned later in an even more anxious state, Alan Francis told her that he had sold all her drawings and would be delighted to receive some more as soon as possible. This was a life-changing episode for Mabel Lucie and the beginning of a remarkable relationship which was to endure for more than forty years. 'Frankie' as she chose to call him, became a supportive and lifelong friend.

With Francis and Mills now responsible for promoting her work, the commissions came pouring in and the artist was able to concentrate on producing the posters, book and magazine illustrations and advertisements which were so much in demand. At the time, a trade journal reported in an article, *Men and Women of Today*:

'Like so many other well-known artists, Miss Attwell has been drawn into the world of advertising and this has given ample scope for her whimsical outlook. Perhaps some of her best pictures are those which are also fine examples of advertising. The red-coated morsel holding a

gigantic Swan fountain pen is one. Another is the well-known Little Miss Vi which advertises Vi-Cocoa. She has designed clever things for the Erasmic perfumers, the proprietors of B.D.V. cigarettes; and Messrs Boots have published her delightful sketches. Two of her very cleverest productions are the Eucryl toothpaste advertisement with one of her most characteristic kiddies, and its excellent slogan, *Your Turn Now, Ol Fing*, and an advertisement for towels in which the drollest of babes stands muffled to the eyes in a large towel, announcing, *Towels is Nicer than Clothes*.'

The writer added, on a personal note, that:

'Miss Attwell, who in private life is Mrs Harold Earnshaw, has delightful kiddies of her own, and no doubt she catches, in her study of them, some of those impish expressions and irresistible poses which are the chief charm of her art.'

This common assumption that Mabel Lucie used her children as models has been challenged by Peggy, Peter and the artist herself. As she told *Modern Woman* in October 1961:

'I never found inspiration in watching my children. They just lived up to the ideas I had already been drawing for years.'

During a conversation with the author, daughter Peggy spoke of feeling some resentment that she was frequently described as 'the chief inspiration for her mother's pictures of cute, wide-eyed little girls'. Publicity photographs of the boys in particular, posing for Mabel Lucie in her Fairdene studio and later on newsreel film in the large garden, were described by Peggy as 'a publicity stunt'. Peter agreed and pointed out that as an extremely lively child he was quite unable to remain in one place long enough to be of any value to his mother as a model. In any case, he would often vanish if there was a photographer around, which explains why the youngest child, Brian, is more frequently seen on film.

In 1911, Mabel Lucie commenced her long association with the highly successful firm of postcard manufacturers, Valentine & Sons of Dundee. Founded in 1825, the company was expanding rapidly at this time to meet the enormous demand for picture postcards right across the world – branches had recently opened in Montreal and New York. A representative of the Scottish-based company travelled down from Dundee to Coulsdon to meet Mrs Earnshaw to ask her to work for them. 'I was a bit doubtful at first,' she recalled in *The People's Journal, Dundee*, 1955, 'artists then didn't feel it was quite the thing to design postcards – but I'm glad I agreed to do it.' So too were the representatives of Valentine, for the multi-million pound postcard business was a highly competitive one in the United Kingdom and, unknown to the industry, with the advent of the First World War it was about to take off in an even bigger way. Mabel Lucie Attwell's association with Valentine was to be sustained throughout both world wars, and produced not only postcards but calendars, books, shopping lists, framed prints, jigsaw puzzles and a most original range of cardboard wall plaques. An Attwell item had instant appeal and this was not just confined to the United Kingdom. As the *Valentine House Journal* reported at the time:

'Prints of her watercolour drawings from *The Tatler* found their way to the battle area and, in this instance, decorated the walls of a certain dug-out. In the course of the hostilities, the dug-out was captured by the Germans who had held it for 18 months. When it was recaptured, the Attwell prints were still on the walls and had obviously been treated with great care!'

In 1913, Mabel Lucie also produced a poster for the London Underground, *Hullo, Did You Come By Underground!*, which created an unprecedented run on stocks of posters and brought her into the wider public eye for the first time.

After forty years of marriage, Mabel Lucie Attwell's mother died in 1913, at the age of sixty-two. Her father, Augustus, went on to live with his unmarried daughter Jess, in Barnes, south west London. He lived to be over ninety years old and was, by all accounts, very healthy, independent and authoritative to the last!

It was in the early postcards that her novel idea of using children as adult symbols first emerged. Her distinctive toddlers with their cheery, cheeky captions had as much, if not more, appeal for adults as for children. This was confirmed in an interview she gave in 1914 to *The Advertising World*:

'My idea is not so much to draw children for children, as to introduce them, if I may put it so, with all their lovable and comical ways to the grown-ups.'

The baby talk she employed in her captions was not necessarily a realistic rendering of children's chatter. It was more a contrived adult view of childhood, self-consciously cute with a very obvious appeal. Consequently, the cards were sent from adult to adult who enjoyed the rather cheeky sentiments expressed in such a novel way. Later in her life she further explained her approach to Charles Hamblett of the *Daily Sketch*:

'I see the child in the adult, then I draw the adult as a child. The situation, the stance and the vocabulary are taken from children, but the message is between adults – me and any other. Children would not understand it.'

In 1914 a second son, Brian, was born. A charming, outward-going, yet sensitive child who was not destined to enjoy the fullest of lives. One year later, his father enlisted into the Artists Rifles and before his thirtieth birthday, Pat was on his way to the Front and active service on the Somme where the opposing forces confronted each other. It was here in 1916 that he lost his right arm. In *Harold Earnshaw and his 'right hand'*, 1917, he described how it happened:

'There was nothing unique about it. It happens most days out there, that or worse. I had been doing patrol duty along a length of light railway for a fortnight, every now and then becoming motive power to trolleys for the front line. Myself and another were doing this very thing when I was 'pipped'. We were shoving up behind, our four hands on the back of the truck and our bodies bent forward like a rugger scrum of two against the opposing wagon. The right arm I lost was close to the other chap's left, yet he was not touched. I was also wounded, although I was quite unaware of the fact, in the leg and back, and he did not get a scratch. Yet the shell that knocked me out burst right over us. I remember sitting up and thinking I was lucky to be alive and I had, even then, visions of a nice clean bed in hospital and a visit to Blighty. I don't think I felt very sorry for myself, but I remember thinking 'pity it wasn't my left'. That was how it happened. A very ordinary, unheroic way of getting your knockout. I often feel that I did nothing in the army except get wounded, and yet I suppose the main thing is that I was there for anything that turned up.'

The 'knockout' to which Pat referred was a fragment of the shell bursting overhead which took his right arm off at the elbow. A potential disaster for a man who, in civilian life, earned a good living as an artist. So, what was his reaction?

'It may seem strange but the idea of giving up drawing never entered my head. The moment I was well enough to hold a pencil I not only wrote to my wife, but put in a sketch of myself sitting up in bed with a porthole at my elbow for I was crossing the channel in a hospital ship at the time.'

It was typical of this determined man to show such optimism. In the months and years ahead he recovered, though never completely, from the shattering effects of that random shell blast. He was discharged from the army as a lance corporal on the 11th January 1918.

Through the war and during Pat's absence, life carried on at Fairdene and Mabel Lucie was busier than ever with her book illustrations. *Hans Andersen's Fairy Tales* (1914), *The Water Babies* by Charles Kingsley (1915) and *Children's Stories from French Fairy Tales* by Doris Ashley (1917) were all completed during this traumatic time. She continued to employ staff to help her look after the children, particularly baby Brian. From Croydon, Joan Coles remembers a Christmas at Fairdene in 1915 when her mother was hired by Mrs Earnshaw to 'help with the baby'. Eight-year-old Joan was entertained by Pete and Peggy. She recalls that they were boisterous children and that Mabel Lucie gave her a copy of *Hans Andersen's Fairy Tales* as a gift, inscribed 'To wish Joan a very happy Xmas, Fairdene 1915.'

In 1919, London based publishers, Hodder and Stoughton, commissioned Mabel Lucie to provide eight illustrations for a children's book, *Peeping Pansy*, written by Marie, Queen of Romania. The artist was already in negotiation with Collins and Thomas Nelson & Sons.

Queen Marie, a granddaughter of Queen Victoria, was born at Eastwell Park in Kent in 1875. She was described in a book review in a Sunday newspaper as a:

'...volatile, glamorous power house, an essentially good woman who entirely overshadowed her worthy, but dim, jug-eared husband, King Ferdinand.'

A colourful description indeed which, however, failed to mention either her writing abilities, or the work of Mabel Lucie Attwell, who was invited by the Queen to visit Romania three years later, in 1922.

In 1920, at the insistence of J.M. Barrie, Hodder and Stoughton again through Francis and Mills, commissioned Mabel Lucie to illustrate a gift book edition of *Peter Pan and Wendy* which appeared in 1921. Although many other celebrated artists have illustrated this story, for example Arthur Rackham in 1906, Mabel Lucie's distinctive, stylized pictures are particularly memorable. Various new editions have appeared since 1921 including a facsimile of the original, published first in 1979 and re-issued in 1991. (In 1929, Barrie donated all rights in *Peter Pan* to the Great Ormond Street Children's Hospital.)

Around this time, encouraged by Valentine & Sons, who were seeking to expand their book-publishing division, Mabel Lucie created a cheery, chubby group of little characters whom she called *Boo-Boos*. The then un-named *Boos* first appeared in 1913 in a series of cut-out books from Valentine. Now, however, the words were her own and in a series of six books, children were able to follow the adventures of these 'do-gooding' elves or pixies, dressed in Lincoln Green, and led by a crown-wearing king. They met up with a young girl called Bunty in the first episode and subsequently lived with her and her mother's baby in Book Two. They also attended school with Bunty, visited the seaside and Honeysuckle Farm, and, finally, had the pleasure of meeting Santa Claus.

The books were a great success and the potential of their popular appeal was quickly recognised by the artist who, over the years, proved to be remarkably shrewd in business matters – not always the case with popular artists of the time some of whom could be easily exploited by wily publishers. Mabel Lucie suggested that some of the delightful *Boos* illustrations would make a useful addition to her growing postcard output for Valentine, if the book captions were slightly altered to suit. This idea was readily taken up and the much sought after cards first appeared in 1921. Later, in June 1926, when she began to design children's nursery ware for the Burslem-based firm of Shelley Potteries, the first six plates portrayed scenes involving children, *Boo-Boos* and animals, each scene accompanied by a few lines of verse. The accompanying teaset was launched several months later – the teapot was a mushroom house, the sugar bowl another spotted mushroom, and the milk jug (somewhat bizarrely) a *Boo-Boo* standing in a coy, saluting pose so that one could lift him by the elbow and pour milk from his head! The model teasets were not produced after the Second World War but

Portrait photograph of Mabel Lucie by Elliot and Fry, c1920.

Boo-Boos themselves continued to flourish through the 1930s and were found on mugs, beakers, plates, cups and saucers in china; plates, the teaset, a cruet set and even a chamber pot were in earthenware. In more contemporary times, attempts have been made to revive the little characters though without much commercial success. In 1986 Hornby Hobbies Ltd., introduced their new *Boo-Boo* range of toys at the Earls Court Toy Fair. Anne Wood, the creator of the extraordinarily popular children's television programme, *Teletubbies*, has noted the similarity in appearance between her characters and the *Boo-Boos*.

Mabel Lucie did appear on cinema screens across the country in one week when both Pathe Pictorial and Gaumont British filmed separate interviews with her at Fairdene. As Peggy commented, '...we were such amateurs at publicity that both films appeared simultaneously.' She also observed that the growing publicity and praise surrounding her mother's work never seemed to spoil the simplicity of their family life. Mabel Lucie was no longer the shy, retiring artist though. She was to move many times to the country but always came back to the London she loved. A capable woman, she looked after her family, managed her career and even found time to travel.

Perhaps her greatest adventure was the trip to Bucharest in 1922 as the guest of the Romanian royal family. Because of the success of her earlier collaboration with Queen Marie in the publication of *Peeping Pansy* (1919), she had been invited by the Queen to stay at the royal palace. Then forty-three years old, Mabel Lucie had never travelled abroad. Her agent and friend, Alan Francis (Frankie), agreed to accompany her across Europe and deliver her safely to Bucharest from where he would return, alone, to London. On the 25th May 1922, Pat travelled with Mabel Lucie to Victoria Station to meet Frankie. A married man accompanying another man's wife on a long journey may seem somewhat unusual but clearly the parties involved saw no difficulty with the situation. They were genuinely 'just good friends' who enjoyed a working relationship. Mabel Lucie carried amongst her luggage a black notebook in which she kept an account of her experiences on the trip. She noted with some embarrassment that on their arrival in Paris, the manager of the Hotel Palais Royal had jumped to conclusions and the couple were shown up to a double room. The situation was explained and a further room provided. Mabel Lucie wrote, 'I detected sorrow on the manager's face!'

The following day they caught the evening train to Zurich and took a steamer trip to a small nearby town. The return boat was crowded with 'over-merry' holidaymakers, one of whom tried to present Mabel Lucie with what she described as 'a bunch of shrubbery'. From Zurich to Innsbruck and an evening stroll with Frankie – he in his slippers and no hat. (The very fact that she mentions this in her notebook, gives a sense of the period. Rules of dress were still formal, and to go hatless and without laced-up shoes was unusual.) A storm was brewing and they made tracks to the river in order to watch the lightning. However, they lost their way and took refuge in a cafe where Frankie, in schoolboy German, ordered tea and the waiter brought hot orangeade, some brandy which tasted of paraffin, and a plate of gingerbread 'covered in ants'.

The next morning they left for a two-day excursion into the mountains taking only hand luggage. (Unfortunately, Mabel Lucie forgot her passport leading to serious repercussions on the Austrian/Italian border.) On Sunday 6th June in Gossensass, an Alpine village, there was a church parade – Mabel Lucie took photographs of the rushing river and looked around the 'quite fine' church with its paintings, tinsel ornaments and paper flowers. This did not interest Frankie of whom she complained in a letter to Pat '...he does not like walking, keeps to the road and is an awful chatterbox.' After lunch she was involved in an alarming incident which in a stacatto style she recorded in her notebook:

Advertisement for Shelley China, *The Pottery Gazette*, November 1926.

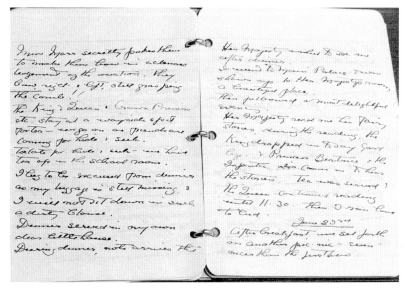

Pages from Mabel Lucie's Romanian diary, 1922.

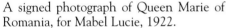

A signed photograph of Queen Marie of Romania, for Mabel Lucie, 1922.

Mabel Lucie in the grounds of the royal palace in Bucharest, 1922.

'...after lunch, left Frankie to have a nap, took my camera and pen and paper a little way out of the village, sat on stone on side of torrent. A company of mountain soldiers came down the road, covered carts drawn by mules, officers on horseback. Band and men. Rather fine. Not so fine as Swiss. After they passed – all was still again and I started writing letters. Rough soldier man came out from nowhere and sat on my stone. Looked at my watch and things. Awfully scared. Kept on speaking to me in Italian, then put his arm around my waist. Afraid he would push me into the river. Managed to reach road where he put his arms around me and tried to get me into the forest, on other side of road. Thought of Pat and babies and home and put up a fight. Wretch started kissing my face and neck and chest and getting nearer that wood, his arms were both round me but I was taller and got hold of his throat and held onto it. Then swung my camera into his face. Down came the blood, his hands went up to his face. I was free and ran for my life down to the village. Narrow squeak. I was awfully scared. Frankie furious. Wanted to go and call out the Army, Navy and everything but as he cannot speak Italian, and no one here speaks English, there was nothing to be done and I am only too thankful to be out of it. Leaving here tomorrow morning.'

For many women such an ugly episode would have resulted in an immediate return home. Not so Mabel Lucie Attwell. The travelling *had* to continue – she had a royal appointment in just two week's time. Ironically, the next day she was arrested for being without a passport. Frankie returned to Innsbruck to collect the document, while Mabel Lucie spent six hours being watched by a guard sitting two tables away. 'A prisoner under the Italian flag' as she described it.

The Danube in Linz was 'disappointing'. In Vienna they went to a music hall where Frankie 'threw his weight about' and demanded better seats. Mabel Lucie told him she would prefer to journey on alone, and asked him to return home. In a letter to a friend in Surrey she confided:

'I would not have come on this journey with him if I had known the type of man he was...earthy, earthy, and his remarks and general attitude to women leaves me with a nasty horrid feeling of depression and sickness...' (however, confusingly, she continues) '...I realise I must accept him. He is so kind.'

On their arrival in Bucharest, Frankie returned home as arranged but not before being arrested at the Romanian border, apparently for having some blouses for his wife in his luggage. Eastern Europe in the aftermath of the First World War was an extremely volatile area, and red tape and petty officialdom was rampant.

After such an incident-packed journey, the rest of her stay at the royal palace seems to have been blissfully trouble free. She writes in another letter home, '...poor shy, little me, pitched right into the very middle of a royal family, ceremony and trappings complete.' While in Romania, she befriended two English women working for the Queen, played games with the Princesses Ileana and Kira, went on extraordinary picnics into the countryside and, at an early stage, met with the Queen in the main palace. This was 'a most delightful evening' during which Queen Marie read out her own fairy tales to Mabel Lucie, the royal children were allowed to stay up to hear them, and the king dropped in to say 'goodbye'. Tea was served through the evening, and the Queen continued her reading until just before midnight. The writer and illustrator were able to meet in this informal way on several occasions. Mabel Lucie introduced the children to the *Boo-Boos* and the Queen, for her part, showed the honoured English guest a bookshelf of Attwell books and pictures. 'I keep them as a comfort for when I am in the dumps,' she confided, 'whenever I am sad, I come up here and look through them.'

The fairytale visit ended on the 13th July. By this time Mabel Lucie confessed to feeling rather homesick, missing her husband, her children, and their garden full of summer flowers. It had been 'a delightful, wondrous visit' and she described the royal family as 'Charming!' Pat met his wife in Paris and they journeyed home to a happy family reunion in Coulsdon. Nevertheless, as always in the Earnshaw household, there was work to be done and commissions to be completed.

Before she left for her trip, Mabel Lucie was visited at Fairdene by the publisher, Cyril Gamon, who suggested the production of a children's annual aimed specifically at the 1922 Christmas market. This was a challenge as it was to be a solo effort but, characteristically, it was a challenge readily accepted. S.W. Partridge & Co. Ltd., of London published the very first *Lucie Attwell Annual* on the 1st August 1922, at a hefty cost of six shillings. The front cover showed a small girl dressed in her pyjamas, sitting astride a smiling, crescent moon, and offering it a rather anxious looking puppy. A typical verse on the opening page read:

'Kiddie Winks, Kiddie Winks, Tales and pictures too, were written, painted, printed, bound – all for love of you.'

Mabel Lucie illustrated the entire annual – the colour cover, black and white drawings, and colour pages. She also wrote many of the stories and verses and this remarkable pattern was to be followed for the next fifty-two years. When she died in 1964, her daughter Peggy continued the tradition for a further ten years.

Throughout her career, Mabel Lucie's output was phenomenal, as she conceded in another magazine article, 'It's true to say that I work very, very hard...'. She was acutely aware of the commercial aspect of her work and never wasted an idea. In an article in *The People's Journal*, Dundee, 1955, she acknowledged that she was a perfectionist, a trait undoubtedly inherited from her father:

'My children look easy to draw but they're not...I do many designs over and over again before I feel they are right. My agent gets cross with me sometimes because I'm so fussy, but I'll only have my best work printed.'

Her newly established collaboration with S.W. Partridge & Co. in the mid-1920s gives a clear indication of her single-minded industry. Apart from the annuals (1922-1932, then taken over by Dean & Son), she also produced *Bedtime Stories* (1923), *Mother Goose – Nursery Rhymes for Baby, Tales for Bedtime, Tales for Teatime* (1924), *Tales for All Times* (1924), *The Lucie Attwell Picture Books* (1924-1928) and the result of her Romanian adventure, *The Lost Princess, A Fairy Tale* by Marie, Queen of Romania (1924).

In addition to the books were the postcard designs for Valentine & Sons. At least twenty-four of these were produced in any one year, and they were proving immensely popular – literally millions were bought at seaside resorts up and down the country. Mabel Lucie Attwell with her bonny, appealing babies, and Donald McGill with his saucy, big-bosomed ladies, were the King and Queen of British postcards although their styles were as different as charm from cheek. Postcard albums previously containing views of church spires, famous buildings and early film stars were now given over to pictures of 'cute kids' and many people wrote to Mabel Lucie telling her of their growing collections. Despite the pressure of work, the artist would invariably reply personally. One letter, dated 1924, was addressed to Kath Blight at Tavistock in Devon:

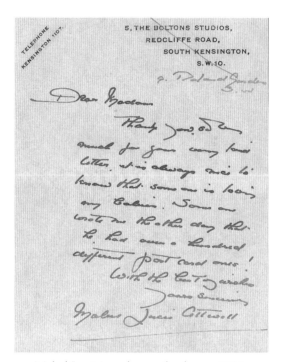

Mabel Lucie's reply to a fan letter, 1924.

'Dear Madam, Thank you so very much for your very kind letter. It is always nice to know that someone is loving my babies. Someone wrote me the other day that he had over a hundred different postcard ones! With the best of wishes, Yours sincerely, Mabel Lucie Attwell.'

The handwritten change to the address indicates just one of the many house moves that the artist made during the next fifteen years or so and her daughter Peggy, in the valuable notes she wrote about her mother's life during the 1970s recalls:

'In spite of producing a formidable body of work, she found time to run a happy home. In fact, lots of them as she was a great one for moving. This certainly gave her ample opportunities to indulge her great talent for making relaxed, simple and elegant interiors. She enjoyed reading, dancing and simple traditional melodies and all of these pleasures would have been part of a busy social life, where party-going and giving were a natural way for a prosperous professional family to make the spring months fun.'

Mabel Lucie in the garden of the Little House, Rye, 1924.

It is, perhaps, not surprising to learn that she preferred the city to the country and needed a wide circle of friends and colleagues to stimulate her work which was always topical and up-to-date. She had her hair 'shingled' in 1925 and, judging from photographs of the period, was a fashionable dresser. Peggy, in her notes, wrote:

'One of her recreations was conversation and she would argue over topical subjects. This was good with her friends, and she liked to talk after parties late into the night at Cranley Gardens and the house on Mermaid Street in Rye. She used to sit on the floor and poke the log fire while she talked.'

In 1923, the 'Little House' in Rye (now called 'Robin Hill') was the first of the many major moves for the Earnshaw family. For over ten years 'Fairdene' in Coulsdon had been an ideal home for bringing up young, boisterous children but now, with Peggy at the fashionable Bedales School and both boys boarding at Seaford College near Eastbourne, a change was sought and East Sussex chosen. At the same time, the Earnshaws acquired a studio flat in

London for working purposes and to enable both artists to maintain social and business contacts. There were dinners at the Mansion House and visits to film clubs and theatres. Pat played billiards and golf, and was a member of the Chelsea Arts Club. They bought their first car, a top-heavy Buick, and enjoyed outings to the countryside. In 1925, Mabel Lucie was elected to the Society of Women Artists.

However, despite the picturesque timbered cottage with a pretty back garden, the 'Little House' in Rye was, in the long term, unsatisfactory. The town itself was difficult to reach from London and the house was deemed to be uncomfortable. In 1925 the family moved to a large, tall, elegant house in Cranley Gardens, South Kensington, and here, according to Peggy, the '...prosperous and gay years began.' It certainly was an exciting time for her. At the age of eighteen she left Bedales and attended the Chelsea Polytechnic for one term before moving on to the Royal Academy School in Burlington Gardens. Here she met her future husband and, in November 1929, the *Daily Sketch* announced beneath a photograph:

'Miss Peggy Earnshaw, daughter of Mr and Mrs Harold Earnshaw, who is engaged to Mr Michael Wickham, son of the late Colonel T.E.P. Wickham.'

They were married the following year but their marriage was to last only eight years. The two children, John born in 1934, and Mark in 1938, were Mabel Lucie and Pat's only grandchildren for Peter was never to marry and Brian died prematurely in 1935, aged twenty.

Church Farm, Litlington, summer home of the Earnshaws.

In the meantime, the Earnshaws had let the top two floors of their Kensington home to a titled lady, and were spending their summer holidays and as much time as possible at Church Farm in Litlington, a Sussex farmhouse in the Cuckmere Valley, close to the attractive village of Alfriston. The farm was owned by Dick Ticehurst who was well into his eighties and lived with his daughter, Jess, a widow with one daughter, Betty. The house had a large kitchen with a huge circular table where the guests took their meals, and a small sitting-room with an inglenook specially for Dick. Several

Mabel Lucie Attwell with her daughter Peggy in their garden at Rye, 1924.

Mabel Lucie on horseback with daughter Peggy on one of their summer breaks at Church Farm, 1925.

Peggy Wickham with her younger brother 'Bill' at Church Farm, 1925. The local man holding the reins is Fred Smith.

years later a rather faded plaque by a certain Mabel Lucie Attwell was found in the bathroom!

The growing infatuation with East Sussex and the Cuckmere Valley in particular intensified, and so the Earnshaws decided to look for a house in the area. Manor Farmhouse in West Dean seemed to be perfect, despite the fact that there was no mains water supply and the only well was considered to be unsafe. In 1932, Cranley Gardens was sold and the couple, with Peter and Brian, moved to West Dean on the edge of the Friston Forest. This move was to herald difficult, trying, even tragic times ahead.

Pat's health was poor but the creative work continued and Mabel Lucie's prolific output did not diminish – in fact, it increased and diversified. In addition to cards and books, she produced handkerchiefs, tablecloths, bibs, jigsaw puzzles, dolls (including the famous *Diddums*), motto soaps, biscuit tins (the first, *Bicky House*, in 1933) and an increasing number of chinaware designs for the Shelley China Co.

In late 1933 Mabel Lucie achieved a new first when she signed a contract with Odhams Limited to produce a weekly comic strip for the 'Laughter and Cartoon' section of their popular family magazine, *The Passing Show*. The first strip appeared in Issue No.86, dated November 11th 1933 and was entitled *Mabel Lucie Attwell says 'Wot a Life'*. For four years this strip featured the adventures of a small cockney girl who boasted a couple of rag pigtails and wore a saucy black hat, perched askew. Ironically, precisely at this time, the artist herself could have been forgiven for proclaiming similar sentiments about her own life. In 1934 Dean & Son published a series of *Great Big Midget Books*, one of which was by Mabel Lucie. These contained over 300 pages and cost only sixpence. Later that year, the very first *Lucie Attwell Annual* was published under their banner. It sold for a mere two shillings and sixpence and depicted a toddler on the cover exclaiming '*Hallo Here We Are Again*', a reference, perhaps, to the fact that, in the previous year, no annual had been published.

Indeed, what a life, much of which remains still relatively obscure. What is known is that Peter, who was a carefree young fellow in his early twenties, suffered severe injuries as the result of a car accident which he was fortunate to survive. He was sent to Southern Rhodesia to recuperate on a farm owned by members of the firm, Valentine. Brian's death from pneumonia in 1935 at the age of twenty is cloaked in some mystery. Mabel Lucie would only say that he died in 'very tragic circumstances'. In October 1934, just months before his death, she took a flat in Earls Court to be with Brian yet, strangely, he died at Ocklynge Manor in Eastbourne the following spring. Mabel Lucie returned to London to a small terraced house in Cambridge Place in Kensington.

The traumas of these troubled times took their toll of Pat, who had never fully recovered from the effects of his dreadful injuries over twenty years before in Northern France. His nephew, Norman Attwell, has suggested that he may also have been suffering from a brain tumour, the effects of which became more noticeable. He died on the 17th March 1937 and was buried alongside Brian at All

Headstones for Harold Earnshaw and son, Brian, West Dean, Sussex.

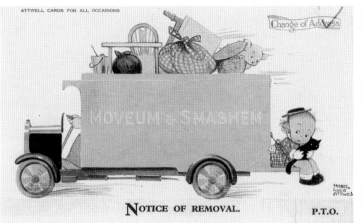
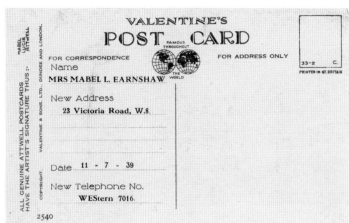

Mabel Lucie's change of address card on her move to Victoria Road, London.

Saints Parish Church in West Dean, close to one of their former homes and deep within their beloved Cuckmere Valley. Pat's gravestone reads, 'In Memory of Harold Cecil Earnshaw who died from war wounds on March 17th, 1937, aged 51 years.'

Following Pat's death and approaching her sixtieth birthday, Mabel Lucie moved into a caravan at Froxfield in Wiltshire in order to be near her daughter, Peggy, who was experiencing difficulties in her marriage. As ever, work had to continue – there were postcards to produce, next year's annual to consider for Dean & Son, and Christmas cards for royalty. In 1937 Princess Margaret ordered her personalised Christmas card, 'There are Fairies' and, the following year, 'Christmas Eve'.

The fashionable Kensington area of west London had always been favoured by the artist and it was no surprise when, in 1937, she moved to a pretty, semi-detached, stucco house on the corner of Holland Road and Ladbroke Terrace. However, within a year, she had moved again to another small house in the same neighbourhood. No. 23 Victoria Road, had an attractive triangular-shaped garden, and boasted a telephone, which met with Mabel Lucie's approval. On the 11th July 1939 she sent change of address cards, (on her postcard design for Valentine No.2540), which proudly announced, 'New Telephone No. WEStern 7016'.

Two months later, Britain declared itself at war with Germany and, with the threat of imminent bombing raids, London was put 'on alert' and so too was Mabel Lucie. There were morale-boosting postcards to produce and a contribution to the *Queen's Book of the Red Cross*, published by Hodder & Stoughton, which depicted a child in a pushchair complete with gas mask and the caption, 'August 1939. The evacuation of school children was carried out with complete success.' At the height of the Blitz in 1940, Mabel Lucie wisely stayed with her daughter in Froxfield. She spoke of this terrifying time in a 1961 interview with Carolyn Scott for *Modern Woman*:

'During the Second World War, I worked alone in an empty building by the Thames. It had been used by the Thames Conservancy Board. When war came, they

moved out, and I was moved in. I stayed there for most of the war. I never went down into an air raid shelter. I was too busy trying to make people laugh about wartime bread and sausages, instead of crying about them.'

Her home in Victoria Road was bomb-damaged in the early part of the war. Mabel Lucie maintained in an article in *The English Digest*, 1962, 'My house was destroyed by a landmine. It also took the telephone.' Temporary accommodation was sought, and for some months she stayed at the Norfolk Hotel, off the Strand, and close to Arundel Street where her agent's offices were situated.

Her final London address was 4 Aubrey Walk, W8. This was a tiny terraced house at the top of Camden Hill, opposite the local water works. The wisteria-framed house was too small to accommodate the family piano so this was moved to Peggy's house in Froxfield instead. Mabel Lucie's identity

A letter from Mabel Lucie's agent Leslie Mills, describing wartime conditions in London.

The Old Rectory
at Froxfield.

card showed her living at this address in May 1943. However, less than one year later, she had changed her address yet again and, this time, the move was more dramatic and would determine the pattern and pace of Mabel Lucie's remaining years. On the 28th March 1944 she was living at Seaside House, West Street, Polruan-by-Fowey. Two years later she had bought her final home, across the water from Polruan at 3 St. Fimbarrus Road in Fowey itself. There are probably several reasons for this move to the West Country after so many years in west London. However, Mabel Lucie's somewhat eccentric explanation in an article in *Homes and Gardens*, 1961, was that:

'...while I was in Cornwall I was lucky enough to hear of a house for sale – the sale to include a telephone. I did not particularly want that house, but I did want the telephone. I got both. It may be a prosaic thing to be the deciding factor and my reason for living in Cornwall, but it is a true one.'

Presumably, another reason was her desire to find a more settled and peaceful way of life for herself and son, Peter, after the worrying war years. She was also proud of her Cornish ancestry:

'It gives me that small feeling of belonging, a feeling which my son shares with me. My father was a descendant of Hugh Atwell who was well-known as parson of St. Ewe Parish, near Mevagissey, in the year 1558, and of John Atwell, the rector of our Fowey Parish Church of St. Fimbarrus in 1640.'

After so much upheaval in her life it was important for Mabel Lucie to feel that she really belonged and was welcome. She spoke of having 'been invited to Cornwall' and of liking the people who lived there:

'The Cornish people appeal to me for their forthrightness and independent spirit and for their strong sense of humour. And Cornwall appeals to me as being an active and busy county which has worldwide interests, and where work can be done in really lovely surroundings and in pure sea air.'

She was also influenced by the fact that, over the years, the south coast of Cornwall had been favoured by fellow artists. She wrote:

'Fowey in particular is proud to include amongst its residents the authors Daphne Du Maurier and Leo Walmsley. The late Sir Arthur Quiller-Couch, the author and Cambridge Professor of English Literature, whose house lies directly below mine, made Fowey famous in his novels of Troy Town. He also was largely responsible for Fowey receiving a new municipal charter in 1913 and being restored as a corporate borough.'

3 St. Fimbarrus Road, Fowey.

Clearly, it was good to know that her love of the region was shared by other influential people. The climate too was a bonus:

'On the average we enjoy some of the best weather in the British Isles. Spring starts to show itself not long after Christmas. The hedgerows and banks are thick with primroses by late February, if not earlier. Our winters are comparatively mild, and it is unusual to experience a fall of snow. A warm autumn generally prolongs the summer season, and then we get a half-hour's more daylight than London.'

Daylight was, of course, crucial. Mabel Lucie preferred working in natural light and chose to create her studio at the rear of the house in St. Fimbarrus Road, facing west. The front windows have magnificent views over Fowey harbour and the open sea, but possibly these would have been too much of a distraction to the artist. So, the boxroom at the top of the house in St. Fimbarrus Road was equipped with a small sink (throughout her working life, Mabel Lucie always used watercolour for her illustrations). This hideaway was described by Carolyn Scott in 1961:

'...Outside the door, in direct contrast to the small, busy room inside, is a plain copper plate: "LUCIE ATTWELL LTD. Registered Office." Inside, only one thing is missing

in this artist's studio – an easel. There is little space to hang paintings on the wall. On the rough, folding table there lies an open box of water colours, several jars of poster paints, and a sheaf of manuscripts – annuals for publication this year, calendars for 1962 and 1963 and handkerchief prints for export all over the world. On the mantelpiece stand two pairs of children's shoes. With square, turned-up toes, all worn and creased and cracked, they seem like a whimsical personification of childhood. Beside them is the plaster cast of a child's head, mischievous and healthy with rounded cheeks that seem to glow through the white plaster.'

Peter Earnshaw, now approaching his fortieth birthday, had moved to Fowey to act as his mother's secretary and companion. The Victorian house owed its splendid views to an elevated position above the town, and this meant that routine visits to the Post Office, family grocers and library were undertaken by Peter powering up and down the steep hills in one of his sporty cars. Mabel Lucie rarely went into the town itself, although she did describe taking a 'long walk down the narrow paths to the sea, and calling in at the Hotel on the way back for lunch.' Local residents today do not remember her getting out and about but they do remember Peter (who was known as the Colonel) and his piano playing ability in most of the town's pubs, particularly 'The Lugger'.

Mabel Lucie Attwell poster for Ewbank on an advertisement hoarding in Brighton, 1931.

Mabel Lucie Attwell in her studio at 3 St. Fimbarrus Road, Cornwall, c1961.

The Pig
Baby

The White
Rabbit's
House

In the
Duchess's
Kitchen

'Oh dear!
Oh dear! I
Shall be Too
Late'

The Trial of
the Knave of
Hearts

The Rabbit
Started
Violently

The *Alice in Wonderland* 50-piece 'Zag-Zaw' jigsaw puzzles, 7ins x 5ins, 2s 3d each, by Raphael Tuck taken from Mabel Lucie Attwell's illustrated *Alice*, published 1911.

Trades people, working at 3 St. Fimbarrus, recall the lady of the house having a rather stern appearance but always with a twinkle in her eyes. Carolyn Scott, after an interview during which Mabel Lucie smoked and drank champagne, wrote in the October 1961 edition of *Modern Woman*, '...there is mischief too in the bright blue eyes of this white-haired artist, whose work is so familiar.' Peter Laurie of *Vogue* described a sprightly, intelligent woman who, '...would almost be formidable if she were not so kind.' House decorator, Rupert Tomlin, doing some interior work in Mabel Lucie's house, found himself singing for her at the end of a day's work. He had casually mentioned that, as a tenor, he sang in the church choir and had recently auditioned for the Carroll Levis Show when it visited the town hall in Fowey. After Mabel Lucie heard his rendition of *The Holy City*, she told him that, with his talent, he was living 'at the wrong end of the country.' She also requested Rupert to sing one of Pat's favourite songs before he left for the ferry back to his home in Polruan. Young carol singers recall being welcomed into the warm front room for a glass of lemonade, although they would probably have been happier with a sixpence!

Shrewd business woman though she was, Mabel Lucie still had difficulty in coming to terms with the changing post-war world. She admitted to Carolyn Scott in 1961:

'I find it hard to understand the world today. Everyone is after their own ends, in search of money. Everything is so extreme. I like to keep to the middle road. I'm still very shy too. I hate having to make speeches although I enjoy going out to dinners and cocktails. But now that I'm slightly deaf, I find myself getting terribly anti-social. One's deafness makes things so awkward for other people. I first discovered it at a Foyles Literary Luncheon. I was sitting at the top table, and there was a very long speech. At the end of it, someone prodded me and said, "You'll have to reply you know." I asked him what he was talking about. "That speech was all about you," he informed me. I had a good excuse for making my speech short. I just said thank you, and I wished I could have heard all he said about me.'

The deafness was, in reality, more of a problem than Mabel Lucie was prepared to admit and she did not get on with the hearing aids which she was offered. However, it did not affect her work, although an increasing number of commissions in the 1950s were taken over by Peggy, including a cover for Fowey's official town guide. Peggy had attended the Royal Academy School in London and was awarded a silver medal for her 'drawings from life'. She regarded herself as a serious artist and was known for her child-portraits, and flower works. The postcard work which she undertook for Valentine in the late 1950s and into the 1960s, followed her mother's style and adopted the famous, chubby signature, but did not quite have the same innocent charm and simplicity. (She recognised this and was fairly dismissive of her work on behalf of her mother.) Peggy's increasing workload meant that she spent a good deal of time in Fowey with her two growing sons whose later careers were perhaps inspired by their grandmother – John became an industrial designer and Mark, a portrait painter.

It was probably to protect the interests of her family that Lucie Attwell Ltd. was formed on the 25th November 1959. Even as early as 1930, there had been concern over plagiarism of her work and Valentine had taken the unusual step of declaring that 'all genuine Attwell postcards have the artist's signature' followed by a facsimile of her signature. Thirty years on, a limited company was considered to be a shrewd move ensuring as it did that 'matters Mabel' past, present and future, would be vested in the surviving families. Today, the family are responsible for the day-to-day running of the company. They have also enlisted the help of a company called Copyrights who describe themselves as 'Merchandise agents for Writers and Artists' and include amongst their clients those responsible for the Beatrix Potter estate. Copyrights has offices throughout the world and is currently marketing Mabel Lucie with a glossy, full-colour brochure which states:

'Mabel Lucie Attwell's chubby-cheeked toddlers have enduring appeal from generation to generation. The developing Mabel Lucie Attwell licensing programme includes collections of ceramics, prints, miniature etchings, postcards, greeting cards, gift wrap, dolls and enamel collector boxes.'

One of Lucie Attwell Limited's successes was in 1987 when agreement was reached with the Chicago-based Enesco Corporation to use original Attwell designs to create a range of ceramic figurines, entitled *Memories of Yesterday*. A collector's society was quickly established across America and now boasts a 20,000 plus membership with its own official newsletter. In 1991, a figure of a little girl wearing a Russian-style hat and coat, entitled *Friendship Has No Boundaries* was dedicated by Enesco to world peace and a special version of the figurine was intended for world leaders. A far cry from the days in west London when Mrs Earnshaw would model her dolls, *Snookums* and *Diddums*, in plasticine and have plaster casts made by a man down the Fulham Road.

In the last couple of years of her life, Mabel Lucie spent less time in her studio and more in a room at the front of the house overlooking the terraced gardens and Fowey harbour. She wrote of it in an article entitled 'I Live in Cornwall' for *Homes and Gardens* in December 1961:

'This is an enchanting view of which one never tires. Whether in the oblique sunshine of early morning or in the full glow of the setting sun; or even when mist rises from the river and only the houses on top of the hill peep over the top. By night the lights of Polruan twinkle from water level to two hundred feet above.'

Fortunately, this was a view she could appreciate from her bed because towards the end of her life she became rather frail. Earlier, she had fallen and broken her thigh bone and the community nurse, Beryl Delve, described her main problem as '...fragility. Her weakness generally.' She was confined to bed where she read several daily newspapers and enjoyed conversations with her visitors.

Mabel Lucie looking across the bay at Polruan from her home, taken by a photographer from *Vogue* for an article in the magazine, c1962.

Her children Peggy and Peter were with Mabel Lucie when she died peacefully on 5th November 1964. In her notes on her mother's life, Peggy described the scene:

'It had been an exceptionally still, mellow day and as she lay with her eyes shut, the pink evening light of sunset came over the water and boats and the little houses of Polruan outside her window. As evening faded, the bangs and tracers and lights of rockets and fireworks began, for it was Guy Fawkes night.'

Shortly before her death, Mabel Lucie summed up her 'lively' life:

'My life has been good and sad. I have, according to many letters I have received, given a lot of happiness to a lot of people through two world wars.'

Her obituary in *The Times* spoke for those people:

'She was a personality of great independence and forthright character. Her continued success was due to the sheer energy, drive and dedicated concentration which kept her at her drawing board through all the ups and downs and difficulties of family life and two world wars.'

Some years later, in an interview with the author for BBC's *Woman's Hour*, Peggy was asked to pinpoint the secret of her mother's success:

'Mother just did what she wanted to do and that was what the public liked. And then she had the drive and application to go on and on producing it.'

Today, over thirty years after her death, the appeal of Mabel Lucie Attwell's artwork is as strong as ever. The yearly annuals ended in 1974, and copies of them are eagerly sought after by collectors; her nursery ware for Shelley China is much-prized and rarely found; her early postcards are rapidly snapped up at postcard fairs. An exhibition of her work was held in Brighton in 1979 and a shop and museum devoted to her artistry opened, appropriately, in Fore Street, Fowey in 1996. Proud mothers who visit the shop talk of their child being a 'Mabel Lucie baby' and one grandmother showed a photograph of her grandchild, Emma, to prove it! The best selling item in the museum shop is the *Please Remember – Don't Forget* bathroom plaque. When we compare the delightful Emma of 1998 with the cheery child emerging from the bathroom in 1930, we realise why Mabel Lucie Attwell's creativity is ageless.

Please Remember – Don't Forget. How could we?

An archive of letters to Mabel Lucie from her agent Leslie Mills and manufacturers such as Valentine and Dean has survived to give us a very interesting picture of her working practice, especially as much is from the period 1939-1941 with numerous references to conditions in London and the home counties during the early days of the Second World War. Reproduced below is a selection, many describing familiar Mabel Lucie artwork.

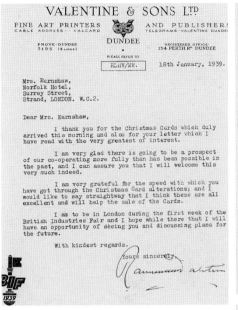

Slogan for the British Industries Fair.

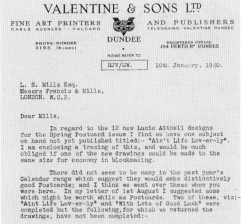

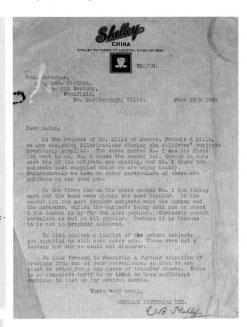

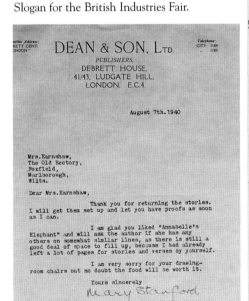

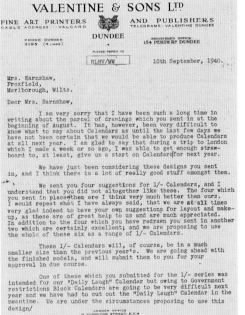

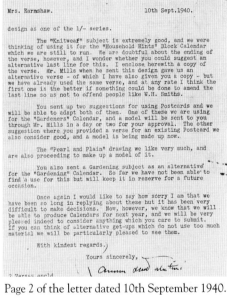

Page 2 of the letter dated 10th September 1940.

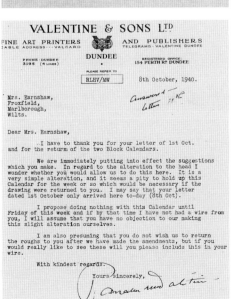

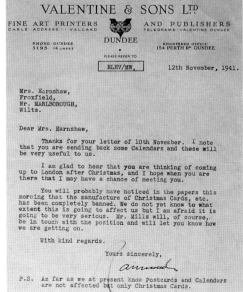

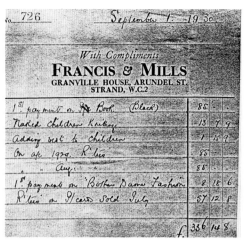

For naked children see Jaegar advert, page 88.

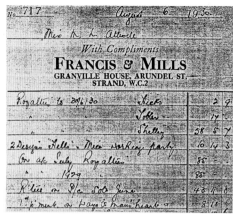

For Ewbank, see page 23.

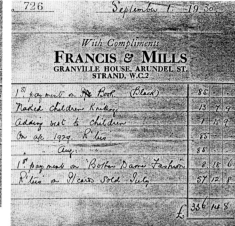

FRANCIS & MILLS
GRANVILLE HOUSE, ARUNDEL STREET
STRAND, W.C.2.

Business Managers for the Leading Artists

TEMPLE BAR 8212-3.   TELEGRAMS & CABLES: "ARTIFRANIL, LONDON."

LSM/CMS

9th March 1939

Mrs. Earnshaw,
The Old Rectory,
Froxfield,
Nr. Marlborough. Wilts.

Dear Lucie,

Thanks so much for sending off the wrapping
paper design and I am now sending you back the cut-outs.
In spite of our careful selection of nine, when it
came to it there were actually only eight, finished in
black and white and colour, but there is a rough for
the ninth which they like. This you declare you have
done but it cannot be found, neither they nor I have
it and I cannot help feeling it must be in the studio
or else when you started to finish it you were dis-
satisfied and destroyed it.

Generally, they want them all finished with
a cloud background for cut-out like No. 2 with a tint
outline as you have done there. I have just roughly
indicated in pencil on, for instance coloured No. 1,
where the outline could some to save difficult cut-outs
round the leaves etc. In No. 3 I have roughly
indicated on the left and right where the cloud should
be continued again to simplify cut-out.

No. 4 will need this effect for finishing and
the same applies to Nos. 5,6,7 and 8. You will of
course also give effect to it when finishing the ninth.
Do not, of course, take any notice of the shapes of my
pencil marks, but they were done roughly in front of
them to make sure I had their meaning.

Now with regard to the colouring, you may
use a blended flesh colour for the faces, and all the rest
should be flat colours. This will necessitate a rather

FRANCIS & MILLS
GRANVILLE HOUSE, ARUNDEL STREET
STRAND, W.C.2.

Business Managers for the Leading Artists

TELEPHONE: TEMPLE BAR 8212-3.   TELEGRAMS & CABLES: "ARTIFRANIL, LONDON."

LSM/ES

Mrs. Earnshaw,
23, Victoria Road,
Kensington, W.8.

19th February, 1940.

My dear Lucie,

I am sending down by hand two of your sketches for the
following reasons. First of all the second "I'se being a
good little girl" was, as you expected, much preferred to the
first, and it is returned with the suggestion that it would be
improved with a pink border similar to 930. They have pencilled
around to show you the exact proportion that the border would
take, and I do agree with them that it would be considerably
strengthened, as this subject might be a little dull here in tone
on reproduction.

Six of your subjects now form pairs for blockmaking, and
here is a tracing for a new subject to pair with "If only
pen could tell". They particularly like 930 as a sentimental
subject, and "Keep it Dark" as a topical one. Mr.Valentine
says that they are all very pleased with the way the new set
is coming along and feel it will make an excellent issue.

I certainly think we might now deal with the bathing suits
"It's nice to be in civvies again", and I cannot help feeling
that we should have one suitable for a holiday maker to send to
a Tommy with some such title as "Although I'm enjoying myself
I'm not forgetting you". What about a wet day one - a wet day
at the seaside always drives people to the shops and they take
advantage of that day to send off postcards, etc. I am thinking
of some such subject as "It's nice to be in England now that
Summers here", with a real pouring wet atmosphere. Ration cards
will still be presumably in full swing in the Summer, and I
certainly think we should have one on these. Perhaps some such
title as "Fido's eaten me meat ticket". I am reminded by Miss
Smith that the stocking question is becoming very important, as

---

Mrs. Earnshaw.   19th February, 1940.

of course there is a big shortage of raw material and the
prices are soaring up. Perhaps a little girl with suspenders
coming right down to the knee holding up short stockings
might help the trick and look very amusing. It could either
be based on "The tops went long ago" or "Could'nt afford the
next size".

What about a girl with a typewriter in front of her
with bits and pieces all around and some such excuse as "If
I could work the thing, I'd have written a letter". This would
do well for typists, etc. on holiday.

It seems a long time since we had a deck chair subject,
which after all is not confined to the seaside, as they are in
every provincial park as well. Are these suggestions any good?

Yours,

Leslie

Page 2 of the letter dated 19th February 1940.

FRANCIS & MILLS
GRANVILLE HOUSE, ARUNDEL STREET
STRAND, W.C.2.

Business Managers for the Leading Artists

PHONE: TEMPLE BAR 8212-3.   TELEGRAMS & CABLES: "ARTIFRANIL, LONDON."

LSM/ES

Mrs. Earnshaw.   14th June, 1940.

Dear Lucie,

Here are three calendar layouts made up
from birthday cards, you will remember it was
arranged that four out of the six 1/- calendars should
be made up on this basis. The horseshoe and heather
ones seem very drab, and uninteresting in colour, whilst
I don't feel too excited about the pink. If you want
any alterations would you please be good enough to
let me know and at the same time put forward concrete
proposals for any variations. If you pass any please
sign them at the back.

I also send the "Christmas Present", with a
sample incorporating the alterations that Valentines
would like you to make. They foreshadowed that your
background was one they would not be able to reproduce
and that they would have to put forward some suggestions
if they were to succeed in making the reproduction.
You will notice that the grey background is introduced
instead of pink. The colour on the upper part
of the dress has been strengthened, which I must say
is I think useful, since otherwise the strongest spot
of colour was the wool in the basket. If you find
any difficulty in taking out your pink background and
putting in a grey one Valentines artists will do this
for you as they are used to this sort of thing.

Will you please be particularly careful not to
handle the rough model, as it is proposed to submit this,
after your approval, to the Queen. Ranald says that
everyone up there is charmed with this layout, and I shall
be interested to have your views in due course.

FRANCIS & MILLS
GRANVILLE HOUSE, ARUNDEL STREET
STRAND, W.C.2.

Business Managers for the Leading Artists

PHONE: TEMPLE BAR 8212-3.   TELEGRAMS & CABLES: "ARTIFRANIL, LON

LSM/ES

Mrs. M.L.Earnshaw.   12th July, 1940.

Dear Lucie,

In reply to your farmyard letter, first
of all thanks very much for the interiors of the
Birthday cards and for the very delightful verses.

I will go down to Deans to-day and find
out why they have not sent you any more material. In
the meantime, it would be a relief if you could start
a few of the agreed calendar subjects. I am sorry
to say that I have had the first real postcard jolt
to-day, which I think is probably a combination of
depression due to the French break-up and the total
lack of trade on the whole of the East Coast and South
Coast. This is the first real low level figure we
have reached since war broke out, but there may be
some exceptional factors which we cannot trace that
are responsible. Your sales dropped from 167 thousand
to 30 thousand. These are comparisons of last year's
and this year's figures. Everybody else's are just as
bad or worse so that we are dealing with a total
postcard flop, not a Lucie Attwell flop. Don't let
this get you down - in fact I think it makes one rather
keener when there are reverses.

Yours,

Leslie.

Viz the Dunkirk evacuation.

FRANCIS & MILLS
GRANVILLE HOUSE, ARUNDEL STREET
STRAND, W.C.2.

Business Managers for the Leading Artists

E: TEMPLE BAR 8212-3.   TELEGRAMS & CABLES: "ARTIFRANIL, LONDON."

LSM/ES

Mrs. Earnshaw.   2nd September, 1940.

My dear Lucie,

It seems a long time since I have seen you,
and I am sorry that when you telephoned it happened to be
my week off. I came up to Town however on Thursday
expressly to meet Ranald, as I was anxious to gather from
him how things stand at the other end. On the whole he was
not taking too depressed a view about calendars or Christmas
cards, but like all of us he was naturally perturbed over the
postcard figures. I discussed with him the missing birthday
card, and he still seemed to be completely confused as to
which was lost. He did not know that you had sent another
one up, neither had he received my letter before he left,
pointing out that the kiddie at the door was infinitely
better than their interpretation.

I hope you are still keeping fairly immune
from trouble your end. The Boche seem to have gone raving
mad about our little village, as we have now had it plastered
with eleven bombs, the farthest 1,000 yards away and the
nearest 120 yards from the cottage. However, it doesn't
worry us much, although it gets a little tiring. They
nearly got me Thursday morning when on duty, when we had
three exploded 200 yards away from us. Now let's forget
the war and get down to work.

Have you been able to tackle anything yet for
Shelley? It looks as though if we are to make any progress
at all they will have to be modelled from your drawings and
then the models checked. I do hope you and all the family
are very fit. The first time we come across any trouble I
will slip down and see you, but there really does not appear
to be anything at the moment.

Yours

Leslie

FRANCIS & MILLS
GRANVILLE HOUSE, ARUNDEL STREET
STRAND, W.C.2.
Business Managers for the Leading Artists
TEMPLE BAR 8212-3. TELEGRAMS & CABLES: "ARTIFRANIL, LONDON."

LSM/ES

Mrs.M.L.Earnshaw. 3rd October, 1940.

My dear Lucie,

Thanks ever so much for your letter of the 29th September, which apparently crossed a letter I wrote you from the Cottage. At the present moment in view of the travelling difficulties I am only coming up every other day, and I manage to do as much or more work by stopping at home as coming up.

Many, many thanks for the Shelley designs. I think they are delightful, and I am perfectly certain Shelley's will be pleased with them. I am not too certain they will be able to reproduce these now, but I am hoping they will. In the meantime you have heard from me about Deans and my letter should cover that proposition.

I am sorry you have had to wire Valentines about the two cards, and I must admit I am rather in the dark myself as to the first two. We have three to carry on with and I think we ought to have an air-raid shelter subject, maybe a kid with a bag of food, pillow, rug, or something of the sort, with some such simple title as "Goodnight, I'm going down below", or better still just "Goodnight", or there might be a subject in air raid shelter dress (Siren Suit); then I think we shall have covered the shelter side well enough. Leaves are open again, and I think we might have something on "Your next Leave".

I note that you don't like the two calendars sent, but do please send them back with your constructive criticisms.

FRANCIS & MILLS
GRANVILLE HOUSE, ARUNDEL STREET
STRAND, W.C.2.
Business Managers for the Leading Artists
TEMPLE BAR 8212-3. TELEGRAMS & CABLES: "ARTIFRANIL, LONDON."

LSM/ES

Mrs. M.L.Earnshaw. 26th November, 1940.

Dear Lucie,

First of all may I thank you very sincerely for your charming hospitality on our visit. I do hope that you will very quickly obtain some household assistance that will leave you free to concentrate on what is a whole time job.

I saw Deans on Friday, and Miss Stanford seemed very pleased with all the subjects except that they felt down there that two pages of motor cars gave almost exactly the same makeup "look" as the last annual. Whilst I know in detail they are different, on the other hand the trade cannot stop and read every page. They are thinking around this. I went for poor Miss Stanford rather hard over the advertisement, only to find that she herself was not in favour, and she said I must tackle Mr.Bradban. Having been down twice without seeing him, I shall now have to put strong protest into writing.

4.p.m. Since starting this letter have received yours of the 23rd instant. A very useful and helpful one. Either I must come and see you more often or you must come to town now andagain, if it is only for lunch and an early return. Sorry to hear you had some bombs on Friday evening, but if you had enough you would get thoroughly used to them. Glad John took them well.

With regard to the booking accounts. I did not book the Princess Margaret Christmas Card since I am still waiting to hear whether this is accepted or not. Only a fortnight ago Ranald told me in answer to my letter that he had no news. I suppose we can charge this whether they book their order or not.

you have put into calendar subjects and which they feel does need to be put into their pictures for litho reproduction.

They are quite interested to consider a new teapot, and the sooner you can give it to them the better. They make a useful suggestion that the set could be based on a caravan, which would form the teapot with the steps turned up at the back for a handle, the chimney of course, being the teapot lid, and so on. For the sugar basin they propose a camp fire subject, but the milk jug seems to be difficult. You will remember that the last one went wrong because it was so rough inside that it could never be properly cleaned. Shelleys are in a very difficult position, since their annual output is only allowed to be one third of last year's, which, of course, being a bad year, was very small. There is, in fact, serious talk about a large number of the potteries closing down on account of the sales restriction.

re. Deans. In view of the attitude I have had to take up with them regarding Kiwi they ask you to replace the present figures, which consist of one head and one figure, with your own. They hope to obtain a repeat order, but I do not suggest you do these figures until that order has been obtained, in spite of their request that you should do it now. After careful consideration they have definitely decided that the two pages of cars are certainly too close to last year's annual and they feel that pages of toys would make a change. With regard to the black and white of two kiddies, No.71, Miss Stamford feels that the doll lying on the ground seems to be suspended in the air, and that the child simply looks as though she is standing on it. As you will see, the feet seem to protrude, and there is no shadow or anything underneath the doll.

Thanks very much for your delightful front page, but Miss Stamford has now found a subject for which we have the blocks, and they would naturally prefer to use it for this year. I suggest, therefore, that we hold your new subject for a future occasion.

Page 2 of the letter dated the 9th December 1940.

\- 2 -

Yes, I just do seem to run into raids, but other people get them worse. I have a 2.ft. crack in the outside wall of the cottage, with daylight showing through, and all sorts of other damage, and it only wants one bomb a little nearer to just about squash it.

I guess Cyril has had all he wants, but then this applies to so many people. We just carry on and don't seriously worry. I think there is an air-raid warning on at the moment, but I am really not too certain, and that is how we get on up here.

So you really have a full house, and I am sure you are perfectly happy, especially with the "two months old", if you cannot manage "It" let me know and I will come down and see to "It". Please give my love to regs and the two grandkids, and just accept my assurance that although two doors away the windows are out, so far we are still standing. By the bye, a main sewer, amongst many other things around us, was hit the other day, and nobody seemed to like the smell at all. Are'nt we getting fussy.

Yours,

P.S. I think the "Blue Bird" and "Flower" designs as a general theme for a set would be excellent and I will see what Mr.Shelley has to say about this. It certainly would be very useful if we had a set up our sleeves for after the war, because we shall then be so rushed that we shall never be able to get through all the work.

Page 2 of the letter dated 3rd October 1940.

You say "twelve" birthday cards - we only have six booked, all the titles of which we have in the stock book with the numbers. We sent six new black and white drawings for the inside, and my impression is that the other six were merely submitted to you made up from postcards and calendars. With birthday cards on which we receive a royalty we only charge for new drawings, taking the royalties on adapted ones. Is your memory better than mine on this point please?

On the question of toffee, we posted this on Friday the 15th, and have the post office receipt, but I heard to-day of a parcel taking seven days to arrive here. Will you send me a postcard if the parcel still has not turned up, and I will claim on the Post Office, for what it is likely to be worth.

I told you I could not remember Cascelloid's last payment, considering we have about 200 royalty accounts I don't think you can expect me to remember. I find on investigating that I raised the question of new lines in May last, offered to go up and see them with designs, but they said that it was far too difficult to consider any new lines until "the war looks like ending". I find that the usual royalty reminder notice went out in June and September, but that nothing matured. I am again writing them. I don't think Leicester has been bombed, too badly, but we do get the psoposition that one writes to a firm whose works have just disappeared and nothing results.

All the best to you all,

Yours,

Page 2 of the letter dated 26th November 1940. NB Cascelloid manufactured celluloid *Diddums* dolls, see page 103.

FRANCIS & MILLS
GRANVILLE HOUSE, ARUNDEL STREET
STRAND, W.C.2.
Business Managers for the Leading Artists
HONE: TEMPLE BAR 8212-3. TELEGRAMS & CABLES: "ARTIFRANIL, LONDON."

LSM/ES

Mrs. M.L.Earnshaw. 19th December, 1940.

My dear Lucie,

Under separate cover I am sending you four bib designs, the first selected, and our clients were particularly pleased with the selection you sent them. They are anxious to have the completed designs as soon as ever possible, and particularly want you to bear in mind when completing that the outline must be definitely pronounced, and as you will remember should be in brown. As a reminder I am sending you two more specimens printed on the fabric that will be used, and I think you will easily see from these the technique that is needed. You will remember the colours are to be limited to six without any half tones, and in case you have mislaid my letter of instructions, the colours are as follows:- Chocolate for outline, and/or other use, then blue, red, green, gold, and flesh pink for faces. They mention two points in regard to these bibs, one is that as far as Gorgy Porgy is concerned you show yellow gloves against a yellow coat. If you retain this colour scheme then the gloves will have to be very definitely and clearly outlined. Then in the fairy sketch which has a cross at the back, it is suggested that you very considerably reduce the number of fairy figures in the left-hand corner, so that a bolder result can be obtained. This Terry material is not suitable for a lot of fine work.

Deans have now gone down to a Rectory in Somerset, and they are most anxious to be able to complete your Annual as they must get forward early since everything seems to be taking longer. I find it rather hard to know which proposition to ask you to put first. I am hoping, of course, that by now the Annual is practically ready. Cannot we get the two pages of toys and the verse cleared out of the way so that you can go straight on with bibs?

Right, Reg Grant Francis ('Frankie' who accompanied Mabel Lucie on her Romanian trip) goes to war leaving Leslie Mills to represent their famous client.

FRANCIS & MILLS
GRANVILLE HOUSE, ARUNDEL STREET
STRAND, W.C.2.
Business Managers for the Leading Artists
TEMPLE BAR 8212-3. TELEGRAMS & CABLES: "ARTIFRANIL, LONDON."

LSM/ES

Mrs. M.L.Earnshaw. 10th October, 1940.

My dear Lucie,

You may or may not have heard that we have had two more bombs at the top of the road, and in consequence I went over to see your studio to find to my relief that for some unknown reason all your windows are intact. I might tell you there is not much glass left around here at the moment.

Three chunks of concrete dropped through my office ceiling and there is a lovely big hole for ventilation purposes. Otherwise we are all fit and well.

I will keep a watch on your studio and if anything happens there will look after salvage.

May you have all the peace Wiltshire can give you.

Yours,

FRANCIS & MILLS
GRANVILLE HOUSE, ARUNDEL STREET
STRAND, W.C.2.
Business Managers for the Leading Artists
TELEPHONE: TEMPLE BAR 8212-3. TELEGRAMS & CABLES: "ARTIFRANIL, LONDON."

LSM/ES

Mrs. M.L.Earnshaw. 9th December, 1940.

Dear Lucie,

Reg is taking up a commission in the Air Force very shortly, and in consequence he suggested, and I accepted his suggestion, that I should take last week off, since goodness knows when I shall ever have any more time off. We went down to Oxfordshire at the week-end to see our grand-daughter, had car trouble on the way home and did not get back to Sussex until Tuesday night. I hope Peggy and the kids are fit and well, and that you are feeling full of beans 'cos I have some work to talk about.

re. Shelleys. These people have been very bad in just sitting on your designs for so long before giving any opinion, but they have atlast done so and I am passing their remarks on to you. I am sending a parcel of drawings and from these I want you please to note the following:- Generally speaking they like the designs but they are not finished enough for their transfers, and when I look at them I must agree that some are shall we say "on the rough side". For your guidance, they think that No.7., the caravan, No.1. the Blue Birds, No.9. the Donkey and Cart and No.3. the Tricycle, are excellent. They think No.4. the Car wants some improvement as it will not look so attractive on china owing to the colouring. You must remember that the white of china is not really pure white, and they feel the yellow car will lack colour. I suggest that the car should be a red one, as this will clash with nothing else in the sketch. They do not feel that Nos. 5, 2 and 8 are suitable for children's subjects. Personally I do not agree with them, except that perhaps No.8. is a little old for kiddies. They feel it would be well to include another donkey subject as this has always proved a favourite. They do, however, suggest that they could repeat the one they have already used, which is numbered 6, and which, I think, has been copied by their Artist for reaction purposes. They have sent us a calendar which I am including in the parcel, showing the extra work

FRANCIS & MILLS
GRANVILLE HOUSE, ARUNDEL STREET
STRAND, W.C.2.
Business Managers for the Leading Artists
TELEPHONE: TEMPLE BAR 8212-3. TELEGRAMS & CABLES: "ARTIFRANIL, LONDON."

RGF/ES.

Mrs.M.L.Earnshaw. 20th December, 1940.

Dear Lucie,

I shall be leaving immediately after Christmas to join the R.A.F. After being in a very happy partnership with Leslie for twenty years believe me it is very hard even to contemplate a temporary break for the "duration". As the younger man I am taking the opportunity of again volunteering for service, as I feel it is a duty, if one can be usefully employed in one of the Services. Leslie will carry on until I come out of the Air Force at the end of the war.

I always think the fellow who is left behind has by far the hardest job to tackle, but in spite of all the difficulties which the war brings on any business, and especially ours, I am sure that Leslie will well andtruly keep the flag flying. In this respect I know how much he treasures your wholehearted co-operation. It is pleasant to recollect the many years we have been privileged to look after your business interests, and may I say, to regard all the artists and F.&.M. as one very happy partnership. May it long continue.

The last war brought Leslie and I together after my father's retirement from the business, andthis war is apparently going to separate us - but only for a short while I hope. In this respect one war did me a very good turn and this war a bad one!

May I therefore wish you the best of luck and continued happy association with the old firm. When this terrific upheaval is all over I hope it will be my good fortune to rejoin you all again.

With the very best of good wishes,

Yours sincerely,

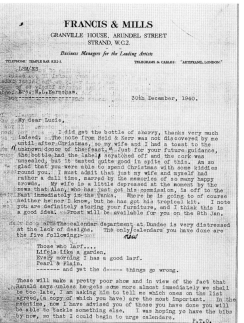

FRANCIS & MILLS
GRANVILLE HOUSE, ARUNDEL STREET
STRAND, W.C.2.

Business Managers for the Leading Artists

TELEPHONE: TEMPLE BAR 8212-3.   TELEGRAMS & CABLES: "ARTIFRANIL, LONDON."

LSM/ES

Mrs. M.L.Earnshaw.

30th December, 1940.

My dear Lucie,

I did get the bottle of sherry, thanks very much indeed. The note from Reid & Kerr was not discovered by me until after Christmas, so my wife and I had a toast to the "unknown donor of the feast." Just for your future guidance, the bottle had the label scratched off and the cork was unsealed, but it tasted quite good in spite of this. Am so glad that you were able to spend Christmas with some kiddies round you. I must admit that just my wife and myself had rather a dull time, marred by the memories of so many happy crowds. My wife is a little depressed at the moment by the news that Alan, who has just got his commission, is off to the East immediately in the Tanks. Where he is going to of course neither he nor I know, but he has got his tropical kit. I note you are definitely storing your furniture, and I think this is a good idea. Frost will be available for you on the 8th Jan.

The calendar department at Dundee is very distressed at the lack of designs. The only *new* calendars you have done are the five following:-

    Those who larf....
    Life is like a garden.
    Every morning I has a good larf.
    Pearl & Plain.
    ------- and yet the d----- things go wrong.

These will make a pretty poor show and in view of the fact that Ranald says unless he gets some more almost immediately we shall be too late, I am asking him to tell me which ones on the list agreed,(a copy of which you have) are the most important. In the meantime, now I have advised you of those you have done you will be able to tackle something else. I was hoping yo have the bibs by now, so that I could begin to urge calendars. P.T.O.

I have put to Ranald your suggestion of coming to Dundee to work, and it might be very useful if you could do so quickly. I will await his reply on the latest date for delivery and which are in his opinion likely to be the best sellers. I think we had better leave the calendar position over until then, except that any one or two you can do will be invaluable.

We seem to be at cross purposes over the Annual. In one breath you tell me that too much old stuff is being used, and then you want to repeat two pages of motors. If you cannot find any suitable title for the illustration sent you then we will have to insist that they make new blocks from your special design, but I had hoped to hold this for another year. I am returning this to you, with original of a birthday card which Valentines have not used. I think these are best in your hands rather than in London. We have been getting it round here rather badly again and every morning after I hear of London's blitz I look up Arundel Street with some anxiety to see if we are still there.

Have at last heard from Cascelloid after repeated applications, that pressure of work, business difficulties, and lack of staff, are solely responsible for the delay, and they have promised the figures in the course of a few days, but that letter was dated December 19th.

All the very best and every conceivable good wish to you and yours for 1941.

Yours,

Leslie

P.S. Am going up to Dundee on the 3rd for the week-end.

Page 2 of the letter dated 30th December 1940.

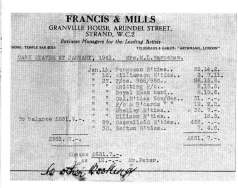

FRANCIS & MILLS
GRANVILLE HOUSE, ARUNDEL STREET,
STRAND, W.C.2.

PHONE: TEMPLE BAR 8213   TELEGRAMS & CABLES: "ARTIFRANIL, LONDON"

CASH STATEMENT JANUARY, 1941.   Mrs. M.L.Earnshaw.

Jan.13.	Ferguson R'ties..	32.14.2.	
" 16.	Williamson R'ties..	3. 7.11.	
" 27.	P/es. 958/960..	26.16.4	
" 28.	Knitting P/c..	8.16.8.	
" 28.	Royal Xmas card..	8.18.8.	
" 28.	Cal.R'ties Nov/dec..	51. -.-.	
" 28.	P/c & B'cards " "	19. 2.8.	
" 28.	Shelley R'ties..	33. 7.-.	
To balance £631.7.-..	" 28.	Ellison R'ties..	18.3.
	" 29.	Cascelloid R'ties..	436. -.-.
	" 30.	Sexton R'ties..	7. 4.8.
£631. 7.-.			£631. 7.-.

Cheque £631.7.-.
Less 12.-. Mr.Peter.

Royal Christmas card, 8 1/2 guineas.

FRANCIS & MILLS
GRANVILLE HOUSE, ARUNDEL STREET
STRAND, W.C.2.

Business Managers for the Leading Artists

PHONE: TEMPLE BAR 8212-3.   TELEGRAMS & CABLES: "ARTIFRANIL, LONDON."

LSM/ES

Mrs. M.L.Earnshaw.

10th January, 1941.

My dear Lucie,

Had a busy time at Valentines, although the time was eaten into rather badly by terrible delays on the railway each way. It was bitterly cold and they had 22° of frost.

You will have had my wire advising me that it is too late for more calendars. This is a great pity because it looks as though it will be a record year, since three of their competitors, including Tucks, have been burned out.

First of all, I am sending you two sets of the last Birthday and postcard issue. I think the postcards make a particularly good set, and the Birthday cards look attractive with the little blue border.

I am also sending you two framed cards, the square one of which is standard mounting and the upright one only a rough specimen. Valentine's want you to go for this market, and as quickly as you can and do for them six motto cards to try and fill a gap caused by shortage of calendars. When I tell you that the upright postcards sell mounted at 1/9d you will see that from a royalty angle there are excellent possibilities. What is wanted is a series along motto lines, or shall we say verse lines. They have been selling religious postcards extremely well with the present serious note in the air. It is not proposed that you should do religious ones, although of course there is no objection to introducing the name of the Almighty if done in quite a serious way. It is suggested that as a layout you should take as a guide the enclosed two subjects, Nos.3100 and 2317. If, on the other hand, the subjects selected do not lend P.T.O.

---

themselves to this treatment then the picture should not take up more than the space occupied in 183. It is suggested that in this case they should depart from the lettering we have been using so long. They would letter their end, and I would get a specimen submitted to you first. I am inclined to think that perhaps a change of lettering would be an advantage.

Air Force subjects are selling particularly well just now and one might make a subject of "I'm so good I've got my Wings", or something with a definite reference to Air Force terms. This could either be an extra or incorporated in this set.

Contrary to expectations Valentines are doing very well, but are badly handicapped by having one small factory commandeered. The rest is working at full pressure.

As a clue to the type of subject for the cards, I am sending you three prints. The verses could be used again but new drawings will be necessary for the theme, as these have had too long a run for reissue. The sentiments expressed in these three are also typical of what we all have in mind.

I was hoping to have seen you this week-end, but I have a pressing invitation to go to Blandford and see Mollie and Mike, my Wife also being there.

Yours,

Leslie

Page 2 of the letter dated 10th January 1941.

- 2 -

done in the right way. We have women porters in the Undergrounds and Railway Stations, and women 'bus conductors. Where two or three people are gathered together the conversation invariably turns to food, especially where women are concerned, as they have the difficulties of shopping; a kiddie returning from shopping with an empty basket might form a basis, or as an alternative Miss Smith suggests a kiddie loaded with a string bag, well over one side with its weight, with all the things showing through which you cannot get, such as lemons, oranges, apples, onions, biscuits, and a grocers parcel shaped like a wedge shaped slab of cheese. The title might be something like "Dreaming of You". I hope some of these will be of assistance.

When I have done the letters I am taking Frost to your Studio and will start tackling that.

Yours

L.S. Mills

P.S. Some game at Studio but will write you to-morrow

Page 2 of the letter dated the 19th February 1941.

NB Far right, 'Harben' was a partner in Valentine's.

FRANCIS & MILLS
GRANVILLE HOUSE, ARUNDEL STREET
STRAND, W.C.2.

Business Managers for the Leading Artists

NE: TEMPLE BAR 8212-3.   TELEGRAMS & CABLES: "ARTIFRANIL, LONDON."

LSM/ES.

Mrs.M.L.Earnshaw.

23rd April, 1941.

My dear Lucie,

It was ever so nice to see you yesterday, and I thoroughly enjoyed meeting you again. I trust you reached home safely without too tiring a journey. Now let's put into writing the programme we agreed:-

1. I think your suggestion for posters on the present empty hoardings is an excellent one, and I should be awfully glad if you could give me a suggestion, Bovril for preference, just in two colours, bearing in mind, although I don't want this to cramp your style, that the white should be capable of stencilling. I think we must have white on black because of weather conditions and dirt. London is full of dust and dirt, as you know, from demolished buildings.

2. I should still like the doll, even if it is to keep in cold storage for after the war.

3. Any general calendar subjects would be welcome for publication next year or later if necessary, but they should prove excellent stock. I am inclined to think that roughs might be advisable in the first place.

4. A set of six birthday cards. I have asked Ranald to let me have copies of the last set.

Each of these is really urgent, but No.1. most of all, or we may get forestalled.

Yours. *Leslie* P.T.O.

P.S. Have just had the March postcard etc. figures. Am very bucked to find that your postcard sales are only down by 7,000. On the other hand your funeral Birthday Cards are up by 18,000. Valentine's now want a dozen new postcards.

FRANCIS & MILLS
GRANVILLE HOUSE, ARUNDEL STREET
STRAND, W.C.2.

Business Managers for the Leading Artists

PHONE: TEMPLE BAR 8212-3.   TELEGRAMS & CABLES: "ARTIFRANIL, LONDON."

LSM/ES

Mrs. M.L.Earnshaw.

19th February, 1941.

My dear Lucie,

I am obliged for your letter of the 16th and am very sorry that somebody's line seems to be rotten, since I hardly heard any of our conversation.

First of all the Shelley verses:- My first reaction to their letter was that the suggested verses just lacked personality and your letter confirms this attitude. I think you have definitely improved the Blue Bird with the word "so". I don't think we should withdraw these verses as I resent the printer making criticisms, and I am writing to Shelley accordingly.

Mr.Valentine promised me that he would have your calendar subjects gone through to see which were suitable as a contribution towards the other six postcards. I suggest that we do three new ones and use three of the enclosed, which are all "Good luck" ones. Obviously none of the calendar titles are suitable for postcards, and you will see that Allen has made some suggestions to convert them. They say that although not in the right proportion, they can extend the background tints in each case and renew the verse or lettering lower down. Now would you like to pick which three you prefer, leaving us only three to tackle.

We have'nt done the onion subject yet; don't be misled by the fact that you have plenty at Froxfield, people in towns and cities have'nt seen one for ages, and there seems little prospect that they will for some time to come. When they do there will be a terrible rush after this gap. Miss Smith reminds me that there is a complete absence of hairpins and clips, which might make the basis for a subject; then there is the "take-off" of women's uniform if it could be

---

FRANCIS & MILLS
GRANVILLE HOUSE, ARUNDEL STREET
STRAND, W.C.2.

Business Managers for the Leading Artists

ELEPHONE: TEMPLE BAR 8212-3.   TELEGRAMS & CABLES: "ARTIFRANIL, LONDON."

LSM/ES

Mrs.M.L.Earnshaw.

25th April, 1941.

My dear Lucie,

Here are the last six cards published which practically all sold equally well, the only one slightly off being "There'll Always be an England" which I thought one of the best. Harben suggests this is probably due to indignation amongst their Scottish customers! However, the difference is only a hundred or two, and is not worth considering.

I wonder if a few suggested themes will be of any assistance towards the next dozen cards:-

1. Rising prices.
2. Hard up-ness.
3. You should have seen our crater!
4. Petrol.
5. Food or Kitchen Gardening.
6. I am not in a prohibited area.
7. What about a girl with Air Force hat, Khaki A.T.S. jacket and A.F.S. firemen's trousers "I'm doing my bit" or "There's Nothing I can't Tackle".

I enclose what was an excellent old one, the title of which I think we might well repeat.

All the best,

Yours,

Leslie

Now please leave the garden alone for a bit. Don't tell Peggy I said it.

FRANCIS & MILLS
GRANVILLE HOUSE, ARUNDEL STREET
STRAND, W.C.2.

Business Managers for the Leading Artists

TEMPLE BAR 8212-3.   TELEGRAMS & CABLES: "ARTIFRANIL, LONDON."

LSM/ES

Mrs.M.L.Earnshaw.
---------------   28th May, 1941.

My dear Lucie,

      In view of the fact that Birthday lines
are making up for the loss on postcard business, I
think Valentines are right in concentrating on these.
They are trying to do so by utilising old postcards
and they hope to make a very attractive line by
fixing on some age numerals. This is illustrated in
age 3, but you will have to remember that this applies
to all. Will you please look carefully into these
and either approve them or amend them, but for goodness's
sake let me have them back quickly. The whole idea
is one subject for a girl and one for a boy between
the ages of One and Six. They have had great trouble
in finding suitable designs for boys, and in the case
of ages 3 and 4 I shall be very glad if you will select
two of the three sent.

      I was to-day in Chancery Lane and a stone's
throw from Valentine's offices found some Mallet cards
in a shop. I bought the enclosed and had quite a row
with the retailer. Am sending them down in case they
may be of interest. All the best,

      Yours

Viz Beatrice Mallet the well-known illustrator.

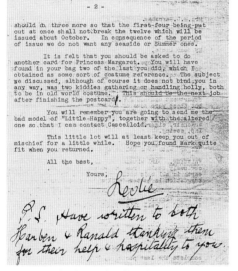

    - 2 -

should do three more so that the first-four being put
out at once shall not break the twelve which will be
issued about October. In consequence of the period
of issue we do not want any seaside or Summer ones.

    It is felt that you should be asked to do
another card for Princess Margaret. You will have
found in your bag two of the last you did, which I
obtained as some sort of costume reference. The subject
we discussed, although of course it does not bind you in
any way, was two kiddies gathering or handling holly, both
to be in old world costume. This should be the next job
after finishing the postcard.

    You will remember you are going to send me the
bad model of "Little-Happy", together with the altered
one so that I can contact Cascelloid.

    This little lot will at least keep you out of
mischief for a little while. Hope you found Mark quite
fit when you returned.

    All the best,

    Yours,

P.S. Have written to both Harben & Ranald thanking them for their help & hospitality to you.

Page 2 of the letter dated 19th June 1941.

FRANCIS & MILLS
GRANVILLE HOUSE, ARUNDEL STREET
STRAND, W.C.2.

Business Managers for the Leading Artists

LSM/ES

Mrs.M.L.Earnshaw.
---------------   18th October, 1941.

My dear Lucie,

      Congratulations on the wholehearted support
of the Powers that Be at the Admiralty and their
sanction to the use as a Christmas card of "Every Nice
Boy Loves a Sailor". We don't, of course, want their
order, especially as late as this, but we are meeting
them as a compliment to you.

      I thought you were coming up this week for
three days, do write and let me know when you do make
up your mind to come so that I can try and keep a little
time clear.

      All the best,

      Yours,

FRANCIS & MILLS
GRANVILLE HOUSE, ARUNDEL STREET
STRAND, W.C.2.

Business Managers for the Leading Artists

TELEPHONE: TEMPLE BAR 8212-3.   TELEGRAMS & CABLES: "ARTIFRANIL, LONDON."

LSM/ES

Mrs.M.L.Earnshaw.
            30th May, 1941.

My dear Lucie,

      Thanks for your letter of the 25th instant,
received here late yesterday afternoon. Thanks also
for the titles for the "jam" subject - there were
certainly none attached when it arrived. I have sent
this up to Dundee at once.

      I quite agree with you that the "news"
postcard was quite the funniest and I said so, but it
seems a pity to risk such a good subject if the title
is not right. It just occurs to me that "OO'er"
would be a lovely title, being absolutely non-committal.

      So you are having your war weapons week and
think you are entitled to a pat on the back for having
done any work - that's fine, I had to turn out in
uniform and lose a Saturday afternoon over ours last
week-end.

      Of course we have stopped the cheque which
you say you have now found, and since I don't know
whether we stopped it in time or not I can do nothing
now until I hear from you.

      You ask me whose china figures are in Newbury,
but I am afraid that is rather a vague question for me to
be able to answer. If you know anybody going in why
not ask them to buy one and the price will indicate whether
it is a Shelley model or a Jap one. Practically no
Japanese stuff is coming into the country at all.

FRANCIS & MILLS
GRANVILLE HOUSE, ARUNDEL STREET
STRAND, W.C.2.

Business Managers for the Leading Artists

PHONE: TEMPLE BAR 8212-3.   TELEGRAMS & CABLES: "ARTIFRANIL, LONDON."

LSM/ES

Mrs.M.L.Earnshaw.
---------------   23rd July, 1941.

My dear Lucie,

      I was so distressed to come back this
afternoon and find that not only had I missed you
on the 'phone, but to hear of your bad domestic
troubles. Poor old Peggy, do please give her my
love - and poor old Lucie, nursemaid, cook, poultry-
keeper, etc.,etc. and you have even produced a
Christmas Card!! I am writing this before the
card has arrived, but am looking forward to it.

      Now let's think of the "V for Victory"
sign. I suppose you have had time to read the
papers and/or listen to the wireless? Harben
agrees that one or two quick postcard subjects
are advisable, but we shall have to jump to them.
Here is a card the figure and expression of which
are almost right except that the two arms should
of course be up in the shape of a "V" with two
fingers extended on each hand to form further "V"s.
I think it would be better if we used the legs
rather than the arms, since we then do away with
the head. What about a rough or two?

      All the best,

      Yours,

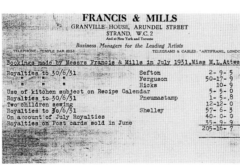

FRANCIS & MILLS
GRANVILLE HOUSE, ARUNDEL STREET
STRAND, W.C.2
And at New York and Toronto

Business Managers for the Leading Artists

TELEPHONE: TEMPLE BAR 8212-3.   TELEGRAMS & CABLES: "ARTIFRANIL, LONDO

Bookings made by Messrs Francis & Mills in July 1931.Miss M.L.Attwe

Royalties to 30/6/31		Sefton	2- 9- 5
		Ferguson	50-17- 9
		Hicks	10- 0- 9
Use of kitchen subject on Recipe Calendar			5- 5- 0
Royalties to 30/6/31		Pneumastamp	1- 5- 8
Two children sewing			12-12- 0
Royalties to 30/6/31		Shelley	57- 6- 3
On account of July Royalties			40- 0- 0
Royalties on Post cards sold in June			35- 9- 9
			205-16- 7

FRANCIS & MILLS
GRANVILLE HOUSE, ARUNDEL STREET
STRAND, W.C.2
And at New York and Toronto

Business Managers for the Leading Artists

TELEPHONE: TEMPLE BAR 8212-3.   TELEGRAMS & CABLES: "ARTIFRANIL, LONDON"

Bookings made by Messrs Francis & Mills in January 1931.Miss M.L.Attwe

Royalties to 31/12/30 Lazarus & Rosenfeld			3- 7- 6
Off to school			31-10- 0
Royalties to 31 /12/30	Hicks		16- 0
	Shelley		76-10- 6
	Sefton		20- 1-11
Design for children's coats			31-10- 0
let payment on :-Mother is this all for me			10-10- 0
I'd really like to come & see you in my car			10-10- 0
You're the kind of girl			10-10- 0
You promised you would write to me			10-10- 0
Poppies are red so are roses			10-10- 0
Of course you know I'm never good			10-10- 0
Royalties to 31/12/30	Spear		7-14- 3
	Hicks		1- 0- 9
On a/c of January royalties			100- 0- 0
R'ties on P/Cards sold in Dec			28-15-26
R'ties to 31/12/30 Chad Valley			31-10- 0
Sheet design			456- 9-11

FRANCIS & MILLS
GRANVILLE HOUSE, ARUNDEL STREET
STRAND, W.C.2.

Business Managers for the Leading Artists

PHONE: TEMPLE BAR 8212-3.   TELEGRAMS & CABLES: "ARTIFRANIL, LONDON.

LSM/ES

Mrs.M.L.Earnshaw.
---------------   19th June, 1941.

My dear Lucie,

      I hope you reached home comfortably, or did
you first spend a frivolous day in Town? Cyril rang
up to enquire as to your whereabouts. Found in my
absence that things had been run very well, and here is
a list of themes agreed for calendars, out of which at
least twelve should be selected. Am afraid our ideas
department did not function too strongly on Tuesday morning,
but these were some of the things we did discuss:-

Domestic Work. Never finished - Trade Unions. Girl in
armchair, cigarette and paper. Boy in apron, kiddie on
lap, sewing.

To the Good Old Days. High dogcart, driver with silk hat,
"Tiger" with arms folded at back, dog running between wheels.

Knitting. Girl winding big ball of wool, the strand
obviously coming from underneath her skirt. "Where on
earth is all this wool coming from", or I think Miss Smith's
suggestion is better "Wool without coupons".

Gardening. Boy in garden with very small stuff, looking
at huge flowers topping the fence from the next garden.
I wanted to call this "You Liar", but I think your
suggestion was "Oh Yeah!"

"Good Luck" You seemed rather to like my suggestion of the
theme "You can't buy Good Luck but you can have it, given
you and here it is".

      Now you have to remember the first job is to
complete the last postcard, but it is suggested that you

                       P.T.O.

FRANCIS & MILLS
GRANVILLE HOUSE, ARUNDEL STREET
STRAND, W.C.2.

Business Managers for the Leading Artists

1: TEMPLE BAR 8212-3.   TELEGRAMS & CABLES: "ARTIFRANIL, LOND

LSM/ES

Mrs.M.L.Earnshaw.
---------------   16th September, 1941.

Dear Lucie,

      Valentines feel that we should now proceed
with ideas for the Spring range of postcards. They
would need a minimum of six and could take anything up
to twelve. Some of them should deal with women's war
work, such as struggling with a stirrup pump, fire
watching, or any of the Auxiliary services, and so on.

      I hope progress has been made with some more
calendars so that you can give them a little rest and
swing-over to postcards.

      I am glad to say that your sales last month
compare with August last year, showing a rise from
108,000 to 217,000. There is a general increase all
round, which looks as though the public have got
accustomed to the new postage price and are carrying
on buying. This is the most encouraging month's
returns I have yet seen.

      All the best,

      Yours,

Some two million postcards a year!

FRANCIS & MILLS
GRANVILLE HOUSE, ARUNDEL STREET,
STRAND, W.C.2.
Business Managers for the Leading Artists

TELEPHONE: TEMPLE BAR 8212-3   TELEGRAMS & CABLES: "ARTIFRANIL, LONDON

Bookings made June 1940.- Mrs. M.L.Earnshaw.

June 4th.	Pottery Royalties -	Shelley -		£27.11. -.
"	Soap Royalties -	B.Legion -		15.11.
" 14.	March Qtr. R'ties -	P.Ellison -		14. 1
" 20.	Book royalties -	Dean		19. 2. 1.
" 28.	Calendar R'ties -	Valentine -		30. - .
"	P/c. R'ties May -	"		51. 4. 5.
"	Numeral R'ties -	"		1. 3.11.
"	B'day Card -	"		1.14. 4.
				£132. 5. 9.

Three financial statements from Francis &
Mills – January 1931 to June 1940.

POSTCARDS AND PUBLISHERS

In 1895 Valentine & Sons of Dundee developed a new colour printing process called Collotype – a lithographic method invented by the Germans – which they applied to the manufacture of picture postcards in the United Kingdom. This established a highly successful method for the cheap reproduction of cards, and Valentine became one of the leading manufacturers in the country.

Two years later, the Government allowed a relaxation of Post Office regulations and, for the first time, correspondence could be written on one side of the postcard leaving the front free for pictures. This prompted a tremendous boom in the picture postcard trade and when, in 1899, further restrictions governing the size of postcards were lifted, publishers sprung up overnight and competition was fierce.

The period from 1900 until the commencement of the First World War in 1914 is regarded by most collectors as the 'Golden Age' of postcards and it was at this time that Mabel Lucie Attwell burst upon the scene with her original and innovative designs. Her earliest postcard work was published by the Carlton Company in London EC1 and also in Raphael Tuck & Sons' 'Oilette Series' of which her *War Baby* in undress uniform is a fine example.

In addition there was the 'Celesque Series', published by the Photochrom Co. Ltd. of London and Tunbridge Wells; Vivian Mansell & Co. of London; J. Salmon of Sevenoaks; Printing Craft Ltd. of London and Mansfield; Alfred Stiebel & Co. of London; the Modern Humour Series; and even an H. Flint, Photographer of Upper Tooting Road, London, who had his cards 'Printed in Bohemia'. Abroad, there was the French publisher, E. Sepheriades based in Paris; Wohlgemuth and Lissner with their bilingual cards in Berlin; Postais Começos and G&F Company of Lisbon in Portugal. Finally, there were the posthumous issues by Angus Sutherland, Andrew Valentine and the Kent-based, Bennett Co.

A senior representative of the Valentine Company travelled south to meet Mabel Lucie and persuade her to work for them. After an initial reluctance – 'Artists then didn't feel it was quite the thing to design postcards' – she agreed and, for the next fifty years or so, the partnership between Valentine & Sons of Dundee and Mabel Lucie Attwell proved to be the most successful in the history of British postcards. For the first four years, the 'Attwell Series' of cards by Valentine, were not numbered. When serial numbers were introduced they were used to indicate the order of publication of the original cards. Most cards were reprinted several times – often with alternative captions and occasionally alternative numbers. We have not included every alternative, nor every birthday version of the cards shown, nor the early 'A' or '7' prefix before a number. We have included some mailing novelty or 'waterfall' cards (containing a concertina strip of local views of UK locations) but these have a special identity number on the front. We also recognise that, inevitably, there will be cards missing from this catalogue of Mabel Lucie Attwell's work for Valentine & Sons. If you own such a card, do please contact the author at the publisher's address with, if possible, a photocopy of the missing card. The author would like to acknowledge the considerable help from Ineke Gockel in preparing the postcard section.

VALENTINE OF DUNDEE POSTCARDS

From 1916, Valentine issued numbered postcards. Those illustrated on pages 33-80 are listed below with the years in which they were published.

1916: 4012-4313	**1929:** 1394-1596	**1942:** 603-678
1917: 4417-4427	**1930:** 1697-1815	**1943:** 704-737
1918: 4482-4732	**1931:** 1881-2045	**1944:** 751-756
1919: 4774-4697	**1932:** 2126-2317	**1945:** 794-841
1920: 105-342	**1933:** 2405-2569	**1946:** 868-887
1921: 385-493	**1934:** 2634-2889	**1947:** 992-1170
1922: 548-667	**1935:** 2912-3197A	**1949:** 1311-1443
1923: 685-749	**1936:** 3277-3613	**1950:** 1498-1670
1924: 795-886	**1937:** 3689-3863	**1951:** 1771-1868
1925: 950-1019	**1938:** 4178-4433	**1952:** 5049-5063
1926: 1087-1188	**1939:** 4581A-271	**1953:** 5137-5268
1927: 1240-1251	**1940:** 391-508	
1928: 1270-1355	**1941:** 533-589	

Un-named publisher x 6

Photochrome Celesque Series x 8

Salmon

Mack x 2

H. Flint

Mack

Vivian Mansell x 6

Some pup - this.

Won't mother be pleased?

Who's a greedy?

He's gone & left me!

You're another - so there!

"Now! Why do they call us a Nuisance?"

Carlton

WHEN THE BOYS COME HOME.
QUAND LES POILUS RETOURNERONS.

Unknown

YOUR KING AND COUNTRY NEED 100,000 MEN

"WHY WASN'T I BORN A MAN?"

Alfred Stiebel & Co x 6

LITTLE SISTER SUSIE.

THE HAPPY PAIR.

IMP OR ANGEL?

"COME ON—YOU'RE WANTED."

BABY MINE.

FERGUSON FABRICS

Advertising x 2

"Skins and tempers smooth as silk, Thanks to Ednett Certified Milk"

'Glaxo' x 2

Advertising x 3

'Glaxo'

THE FROG PRINCE

Raphael Tuck x 9

LITTLE RED RIDING HOOD

HANSEL AND GRETHEL

THE GOLDEN GOOSE

THE STEADFAST TIN SOLDIER

THE SOLDIER AND THE WITCH (From "The Tinder Box.")

THE CHANGELING

SNOW-WHITE AND ROSE-RED

CHRISTMAS GREETINGS

THE WAR BABY

It's aye guid for Luck, but ye canna sit on a thistle!

U NASTY BOAT!

I'LL MEND YOUR HEART FOR YOU!

1er Avril

I'VE A HEART FOR YOU DEAR!

O! SEE WHAT YOU'VE DONE TO MY HEART

Let's be lovers, you and me, Like the bigger folks we see.

I give you a kiss I will be very strange If you don't give to me A kiss in exchange

I'M shy, my dear, but I'd like you to know My heart has been stricken by Cupid's bow.

As I love you, if you'd love me, Why, what a lot of love there'd be!

I wonder if you know who loves you well! Because if you can guess, I needn't tell.

LOVING EASTER GREETINGS

TO WISH YOU A HAPPY EASTER

A Happy Easter

EASTER GREETINGS

LOVING EASTER GREETINGS

EASTER GREETINGS

To wish you A Happy Easter

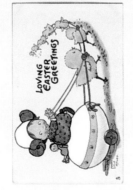

LOVING EASTER GREETINGS

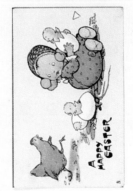

A HAPPY EASTER

Vroolijk Paaschfeest

Rapahel Tuck x 10

Valentine x15

"I'se so worry sorry"

Have you seen any Germans?

Who's little brudder are oo?

An Anxious Moment.

Whad a big bath!

I'se frightened!

ADRIFT

Mixed Bathing
He won't come clean!

Mixed Bathing
Why won't oo kiss me!

Mixed Bathing
He won't come clean!

Mixed Bathing
Hand Over Below!

Mixed Bathing
Ready?

Mixed Bathing
I feels all shy

"Is it cold?"

"Who's afraid?"

"Oar! Dear it"

"Two's Company!"

"Please, Mr Crab, go home!"

"Mary Jane must learn to swim!"

Dreadful Weather

To the Rescue!

Drifting out to Sea!

Just a Line from BOGNOR

Ise not afraid
of the Germans

Rule Britannia.

JUST A LINE FROM CLIFTONVILLE

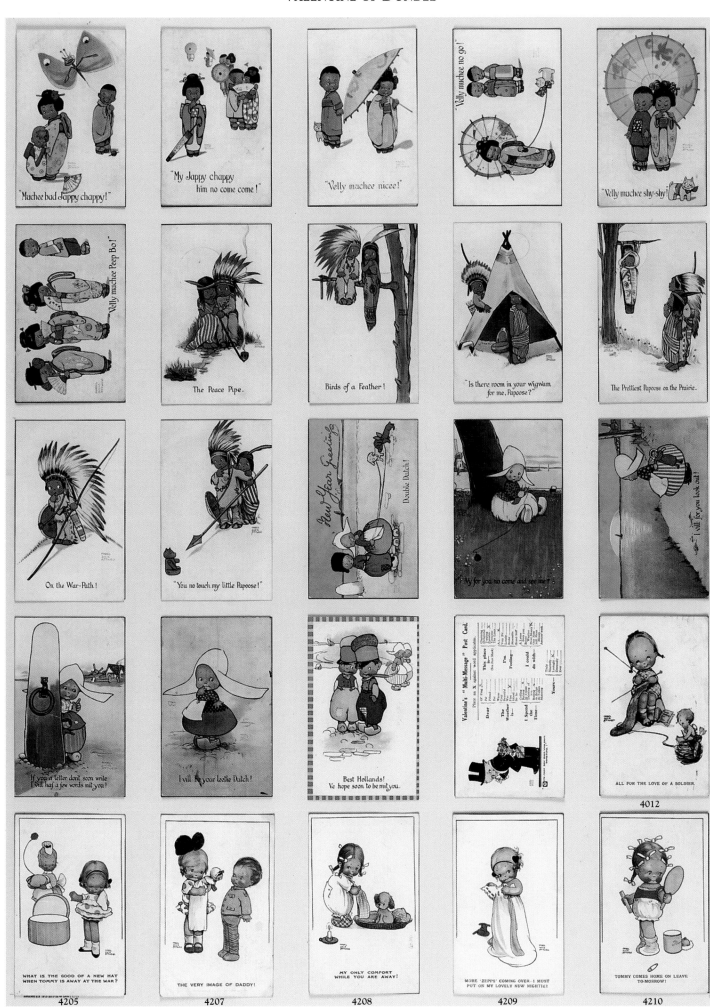

"Muchee bad Jappy chappy!"

"My Jappy chappy him no come come!"

"Velly muchee nicee!"

"Velly muchee no go!"

"Velly muchee shy-shy!"

"Velly muchee Peep Bo!"

The Peace Pipe.

Birds of a Feather!

"Is there room in your wigwam for me, Papoose?"

The Prettiest Papoose on the Prairie.

On the War-Path!

"You no touch my little Papoose!"

New Year Greeting

Double Dutch!

"My for you no come and see me?"

I vill for you look out!

If you a letter dont soon write I vill haf a few words mit you!

I vill be your leetle Dutch!

Best Hollands! Ve hope soon to be mit you.

Valentine's "Multi-Message" Post Card.

ALL FOR THE LOVE OF A SOLDIER.

4012

WHAT IS THE GOOD OF A NEW HAT WHEN TOMMY IS AWAY AT THE WAR?

THE VERY IMAGE OF DADDY!

MY ONLY COMFORT WHILE YOU ARE AWAY!

MORE 'ZEPPS' COMING OVER—I MUST PUT ON MY LOVELY NEW NIGHTIE!

TOMMY COMES HOME ON LEAVE TO-MORROW!

4205

4207

4208

4209

4210

39

"PUT OUT THAT LIGHT"

4305

WAR ECONOMY!—
WHERE'S DADDY'S BEST COAT?
I WANT TO MAKE A KETTLE HOLDER!

4306

I WAS A GOOD 'ITTLE GIRL
TILL I MET YOU!

4308

MY BIRTHDAY COSTUME!

4313

WE'S NOT AFRAID OF THE DARK!

4417

IF I WERE THE ONLY GIRL
IN THE WORLD?

4418

SHALL US? LET'S!

4419

THE END OF A PERFECT DAY.

4420

ALL DRESSED UP AND NO PLACE
TO GO.

4421

WHO'S AFRAID OF THE DARK?

4422

THEN I WOKE UP.
SOME DREAM.

4423

THE BOY WHO STOLE A WHOLE
LUMP OF SUGAR.

4424

A SIGN OF PEACE.

4425

IT'S UP TO YOU, DEAR!

4426

READY WHEN YOU ARE!

4427

WHAT
NEXT?

4482

I WONDER IF YOU MISS ME
SOMETIMES?

4483

COME INTO THE OFFICE!

4485

I'SE STARTED MY BOTTOM DRAWER!

4486

I DON'T ZINK I LOOK OVERDRESSED!

4487

NOTHING DOING!

4488

YOU ARE VERY FOND OF THE BOYS!

4490

CHEERIO! STILL GOT SOME PUDDEN.

4496

I DON'T WANT TO LEAVE THIS PLACE.

4497

I'LL GIVE YOU SOCKS IF YOU
DON'T WRITE

4498

40

THE BOY WHO EXCEEDED HIS FOOD RATIONS.

4508

HUSH!
Chut!

4546

SONNY

4547

STRAVAGENCE!
"WONDER WHERE MUVVER BOUGHT IT!"

4548

THERE'S LOTS OF BOYS ABOUT, 'TIS TRUE, BUT NOT A SINGLE ONE, LIKE YOU.

4584

GET READY! IT'S YOUR TURN NEXT!

4585

WHAT'S A NEW HAT TO ME WITH YOU SO FAR AWAY!

4586

I MEAN TO KEEP SWEET WITH YOU.

4588

ALL FOR THE LOVE OF SOMEBODY

4589

MOTHER TO "BAIRN'S FATHER": "WELL, IF YOU KNOW A BETTER 'OME 'GO TO IT!"

4590

KISS ME! I'LL KEEP IT DARK.

4591

BOBBED.

4603

LUCKY DOG!

4604

"I DON'T WANT TO LEAVE YOU BUT I THINK I OUGHT TO GO."

4645

SEE WHAT SANTA CLAUS BROUGHT MUVVER.

4667

THE BROKEN DOLL

4686

S.O.S.

4687

A PROBLEM IN RECONSTRUCTION.

4691

THE SONG OF THE SEA.

4697

SECRETS.

4699

I MAY NOT BE GOOD LOOKING BUT I AM GOOD.

4702

I FINK I'LL BE AN OLD MAID AFTER ALL.

4703

OFF TO THE SEASIDE.

4704

I LOVE A LASSIE!

4706

WHERE'S MUVVER?

4731

FIDO'S SWALLOWED OUR FARTHING!	ALL FOR THE LOVE OF A LADDIE!	SUGAR AND SPICE AN ALL THINGS NICE THAT'S WHAT LITTLE GIRLS ARE MADE OF!	ISN'T HE SWEET?	I'SE SUCH A GOOD LITTLE GIRL— SOMETIMES!
4732	4774	4785	4810	4811
MITHER'S WEE BIT LADDIE!	THEY FINKS I'SE GOING TO SLEEP!	FROM HIM!	THE BRIDE—GOD BLESS HER! THE BRIDEGROOM—GOD HELP HIM!	AND ANOTHER LITTLE "BIT" WON'T DO HER ANY HARM.
4812	4813	4814	4815	4816
TAKING AFTER MOTHER	NOBODY LOVES ME!	OO-MY! CAN'T OO FLY?	FIRST LOVE.	SEE WHAT MUVVER FOUND UNDER THE GOOSEBERRY BUSH!
4932	4933	4934	4935	4969
I'LL CUT YOU OFF MY LIST OF FRIENDS IF YOU DON'T WRITE ME SOON.	A... Birthday Greeting — I fink with all this pudding here You'll have a happy Birfday dear.	SHALL US? LET'S!	THE STUFF TO GIVE 'EM	
105	173M	222	224	
"IT!"	NOW HE CAN'T SAY I'SE A FLAPPER	PALS.	I LIKES OO!	AND YOU'RE ANOTHER-SO THERE
309	310	311	328	329

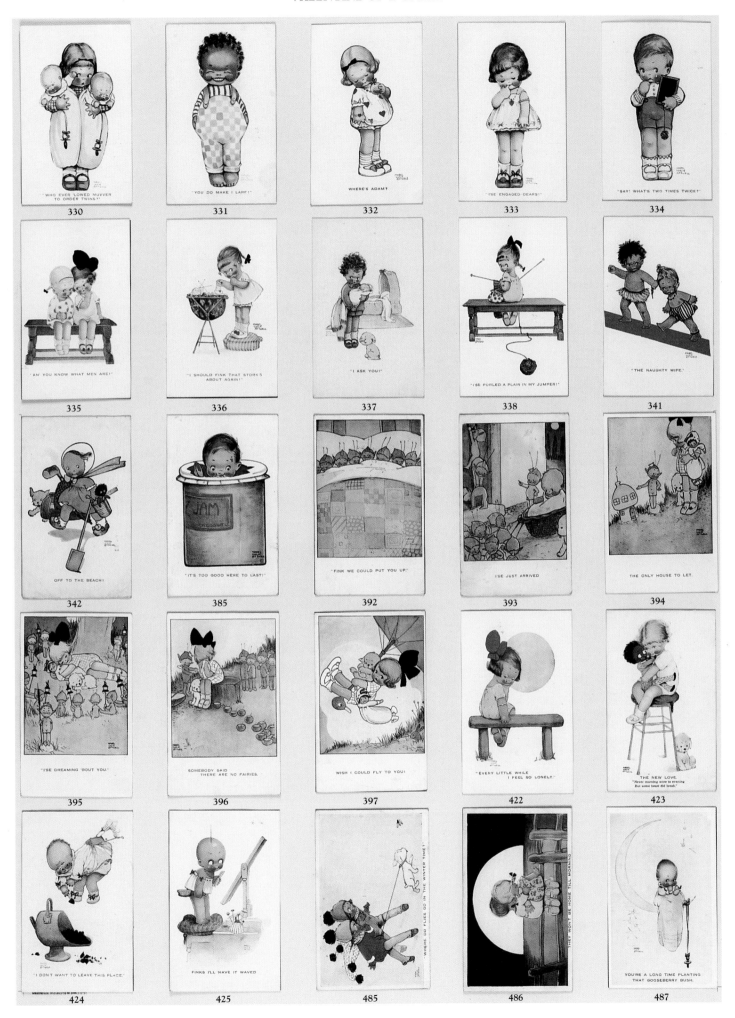

330 — "WHO EVER 'LOWED MUVVER TO ORDER TWINS?"

331 — "YOU DO MAKE I LARF!"

332 — WHERE'S ADAM?

333 — "I'SE ENGAGED DEARS!"

334 — "SAY! WHAT'S TWO TIMES TWICE?"

335 — "AN' YOU KNOW WHAT MEN ARE!"

336 — "I SHOULD FINK THAT STORKS ABOUT AGAIN!"

337 — "I ASK YOU!"

338 — "I'SE PURLED A PLAIN IN MY JUMPER!"

341 — "THE NAUGHTY WIFE."

342 — OFF TO THE BEACH!

385 — "IT'S TOO GOOD HERE TO LAST!"

392 — "FINK WE COULD PUT YOU UP."

393 — I'SE JUST ARRIVED

394 — THE ONLY HOUSE TO LET.

395 — "I'SE DREAMING 'BOUT YOU."

396 — SOMEBODY SAID THERE ARE NO FAIRIES.

397 — WISH I COULD FLY TO YOU!

422 — "EVERY LITTLE WHILE I FEEL SO LONELY."

423 — THE NEW LOVE. "Never morning wore to evening But some heart did break."

424 — "I DON'T WANT TO LEAVE THIS PLACE."

425 — FINKS I'LL HAVE IT WAVED

485 — WHERE DO FLIES GO IN THE WINTER TIME?

486 — THEY WON'T BE HOME TILL MORNING

487 — YOU'RE A LONG TIME PLANTING THAT GOOSEBERRY BUSH.

"I'LL LEARN 'EM
TO LEARN ME MUSIC!"
488

"THAT'S THE WORST OF THEM
CHEAP SOCKS!"
489

DO PLEASE WRITE!
490

"SOMETIMES I FINKS
YOU DON'T QUITE LOVE ME!"
491

I FINK HE SEES ME!
492

THANK GOD FOR FARVER!
Pour faire comme papa!
493

MY OLD DUTCH.
548

WHEN YOU DO GET A LITTLE BIT
OF LUCK, HANG ON TO IT.
549

STRIKES ME, ME'S YOUR MATCH!
550

SWEET HONEYMOON
561

BLACK CATS MAY BE LUCKY—
BUT I WISH YOU'D KEEP 'EM!
562

To Greet your Birthday
TO WISH YOU A SWEET
AND HAPPY TIME
FROM EARLY MORN
TILL EVENING CHIME
563

Birthday Wishes
WE'S COME TO WISH, DEAR,
THAT YOU MAY
HAVE EVERY HAPPINESS TO-DAY.
564

OH! GOLLY! HOW I LOVE YOU!
579

ANOTHER LITTLE LADDIE
WON'T DO YOU ANY HARM
591

ANOTHER LITTLE LASSIE
WON'T DO YOU ANY HARM!
592

IT'S YOURSELF
THAT I'M BRINGING GOOD LUCK!
593

O, HELP!
614

YOU SHOULD HAVE HEARD HIM!!
615

616

DO BE FRIENDS WIF ME.
617

651

"SEE WHAT I'SE BROUGHT YOU FROM FAIRYLAND!"
652

STAR FISHING
653

654

655	656	657	658	659
661	662	663	664	665
666	667	685	686	687
688	689	691	692	694
695	696	697	698	699

740

741

745 I LOVES BEING ALIVE, I DOES.

746 I'VE A GREAT BIG WISH TO SEE YOU SOON.

747 I'M HOPING TO SEE YOU SOON.

748 HOW TIME FLIES.

749 DAILY MAIL WHAT TO DO WITH OUR SUPERFLUOUS WOMEN

795 AFTER THE JOLLY OL' BALL.

796 I DO LOVE YOU SO.

797 I'M SO SORRY DEAR!

798 CHEERIO—OL' FING!

799 THE FIRST WASHING.

800 "A CHIP OF THE OLD BLOCK."

801 MAY EVERYTHING GO WITH A SWING!

802 WE'S HAPPY! HOW'S YOURSELF? On we live fast fast!

803 EVER BEEN HAD?

804 ALL OVER SHY LIKE!

805 A LAPFUL OF LUCK.

805 SOLUTION LOTHS OF LUCK

806

807 THE BLUES.

808 YES—MUVVER CAN GO TO THE PICTURES NOW!

809 OH! UNCLE!!

809 SOLUTION

810 WHAT ARE THE AIR-WAVES SAYING?

811 — ROSEMARY— THAT'S FOR REMEMBRANCE DEAR.

812 — 'SCUSE MY BACK.

839 — I'SE COME TO - WISH YOU A MERRY CHRISTMAS.

880 — SEND ALL LIFE'S LITTLE WORRIES SKIPPING.

881 — CHEERIO! HERE'S LUCK.

882 — WIF LOVE AND KISSES.

883 — A LAUGH A DAY KEEPS MISFORTUNE AWAY.

883 — SOLUTION.

884 — LUCK AT LAST—HE LOVES ME!

885 — "THANK GOD FOR FIDO."

886 — Birthday Greetings — I LIKES 'OO, DEAR, THAT'S WHY I SEND THIS CARD TO WISH YOU JOY NO END

950 — I AIN'T NOBODY'S DARLING!

951 — EVERYBODY'S LOVED BY SOMEONE.

952 — SOMETHING'S BUST.

953 — FORGET-ME-NOT, DEAR.

954 — 'SPECS TO SEE YOU SOON, DEAR.

955 — TOO SHY FOR WORDS.

957 — DETAINED AT THE OFFICE!

958 — US!

959 — FINKS I COULD GET MARRIED NOW?

973 — "WONDERFUL ONE!"

974 — I'SE BEEN BOBBED AND I'SE BEEN SHINGLED, NOW I'SE MIXED 'EM BOTH AND SINGLED! LIFE IS FULL OF WEAR AND TEAR DOING OF MY—BLARSTED HAIR!!

975 — I'LL FLY ALONG TO SEE YOU SOON.

976 — AN' WHEN I FINKS ABOUT YOU, DEAR, MY HEART'S ALL SAD BECOS YOU DO NOT SEEM TO BE TO ME JUST LIKE YOU USED TO WAS.

977 — THEM LAUNDRIES!

47

1091

1092

1093

1094

1095

1096

1097

1098

1099

1170

1171

1172

1173

1174

1175

1176

1177

1178

1179

1180

1181

1182

1183

1184

1185

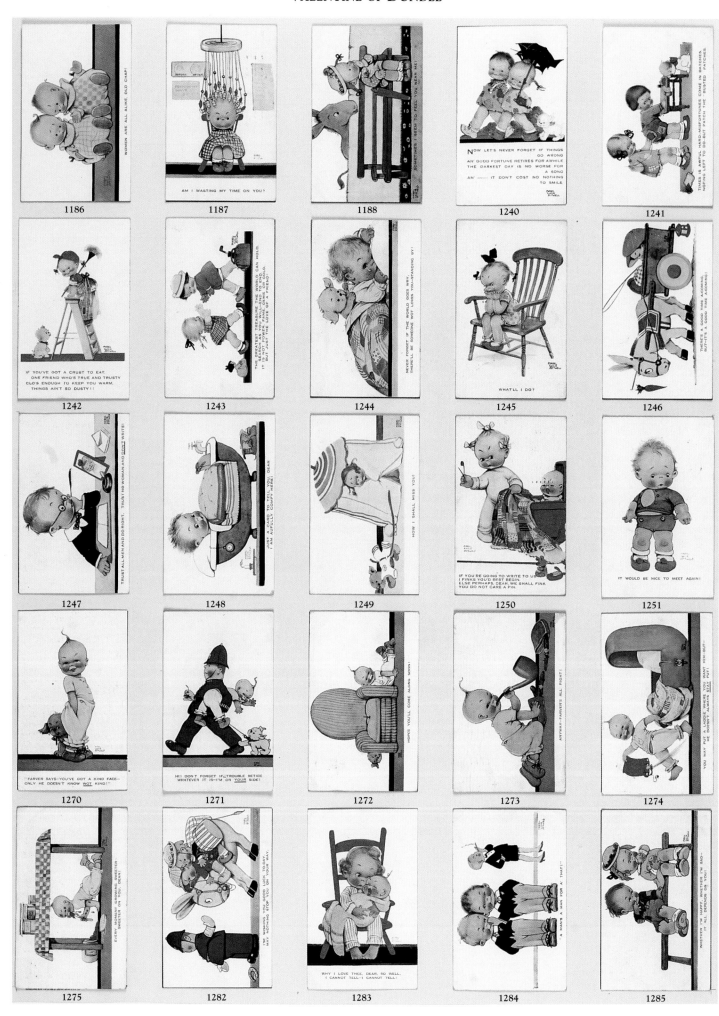

1186   1187   1188   1240   1241

1242   1243   1244   1245   1246

1247   1248   1249   1250   1251

1270   1271   1272   1273   1274

1275   1282   1283   1284   1285

1589

1590

1591

1592

1593

1594

1595

1596

1697

1698

1699

1700

1701

1702

1703

1704

1705

1706

1707

1708

1761

1762

1763

1764

1765

1766

1773

1774

1775

1801

1802

1803

1804

1805

1806

1807

1808

1809

1810

1811

1812

1813

1814

1815

1881

1890

1891

1892

1893

1894

1895   1896   1897   1898   1899

1900   1901   1956   1957   1958

1959   1960   1961   1962   1963

1987   1988   1990   1991   2028

2029   2030   2031   2032   2033

2034

2035

2036

2037

2038

2039

2040

2041

2042

2043

2044/2240

2045

2126

2127

2128

2129

2130

2131

2132

2133

2134

2135

2136

2137

2138

2139

2140/2141

2142

2187

2188

2189

2190

2191

2192

2235

2238

2239

2241

2242

2243

2244

2245

2246

2301

2302

2303

2304

2305

2306

2307

2308

2309

2310

2311

2312

2313

2314

2315

2316

2317

2405

2406

2407

2408

2409

2410

2411

2412

2413

2414

2415

2416

2417

2418

2419

2543

2548

2550

2551

2552

2553

2554

2555

2558

2561

2562

2565

2566

2567

2568

2569

2634

2640

2641

2642

2643

2644

2645

2646

2647

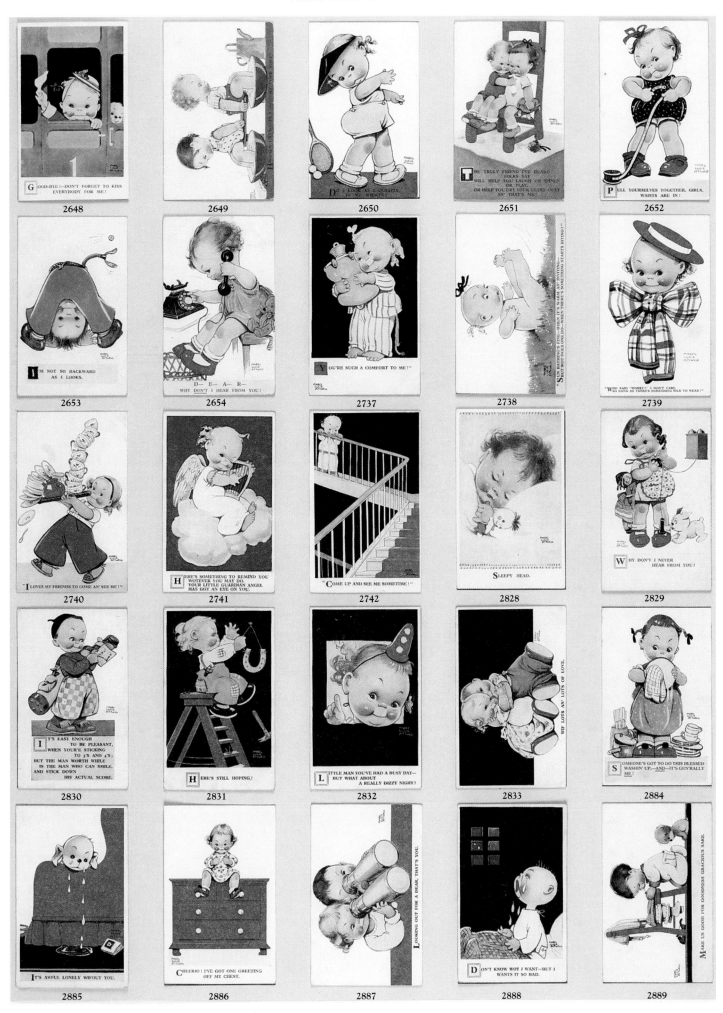

2648   2649   2650   2651   2652

2653   2654   2737   2738   2739

2740   2741   2742   2828   2829

2830   2831   2832   2833   2884

2885   2886   2887   2888   2889

2912

2913

2914

2915

2916

2917

2918

2919

2920

2921

2922

2923

2924

2925

2926

3021

3022

3023

3024

3025

3026

3098

3099

3100

3101

BUT WHY THIS SILLY "STORK" ABOUT A STORK?

3102

WHAT ABOUT A NICE LITTLE WEEK-END?

3103

NUFFING EVER COMES OFF WIF ME—'CEPT BUTTONS!

3104

IN THESE DAYS OF "GETTING" AN' "SHOVING" DO LEAVE A BIT OF TIME FOR LOVING!

3105

MAKE A LITTLE GARDEN GAY IN THE HOPE THAT P'RAPS IT MAY CHEER SOMEBODY ON THE WAY!

3106

ME WANTS TO BE YOUR TRULY FRIEND!

3107

WOT'S SO NICE ABOUT A CAR?—IT BRINGS YOU HERE FROM WHERE YOU ARE.

3109

ALL DRESSED UP AN' NOWHERE TO GO.

3197A

DID YOU KNOW I'M ALSO A GOOD COOK?

3277

YOU CAN'T DO THAT THERE HERE.

3278

UP THE WOODEN HILL TO BEDFORDSHIRE.

3279

I DON'T LIKE THE NUDIST CRAZE— "WEAR JUST WOT YOU START IN"— NO—I THINK THE WORLD'S THE PLACE WE SHOULD ALL BE SMART IN.

3280

OH!—LOOK AT ME LOOKING AT YOU.

3281

MAY YOUR FLOWERS BE EVEN BETTER THAN THE PICTURES ON THE PACKETS

3282

GEN'RALLY SPEAKING—WOMEN ARE GEN'RALLY SPEAKING.

3283

HAPPY DAYS.

3284

DON'T FORGET I'M EXPECTIN' YOU.

3285

WOTEVER HAPPENS OL'E DEAR TO YOU, YOU'LL FIND IN ME A FRIEND WOT'S TRUE.

3286

IT'S HARD TO LIVE WITHIN ONE'S INCOME BUT IT'S HARDER TO LIVE WITHOUT IT.

3287

HERE AM I—BUT WHERE ARE YOU? Me voilà bien triste dans ma solitude!

3353

HOW AM I DOIN'?

3354

HI! WHO'S STUCK A PIN IN ME INDIARUBBER GEE?

3355

FARVER SAYS A MAN CAN ALWAYS TELL A LADY—— BUT——WOT DO WE TELL 'EM?

3356

HERE'S SOMETHING TO BE GOING ON WIF!

3358

"WHY DO YOU PLAY THIS GOLF?" SAYS SHE "TO KEEP MESELF FIT, OF COURSE!" SAYS HE. "FIT FOR WOT, PRAY SAY?" SAYS SHE "FIT TO PLAY GOLF, OL'E DEAR!" SAYS HE.

3389

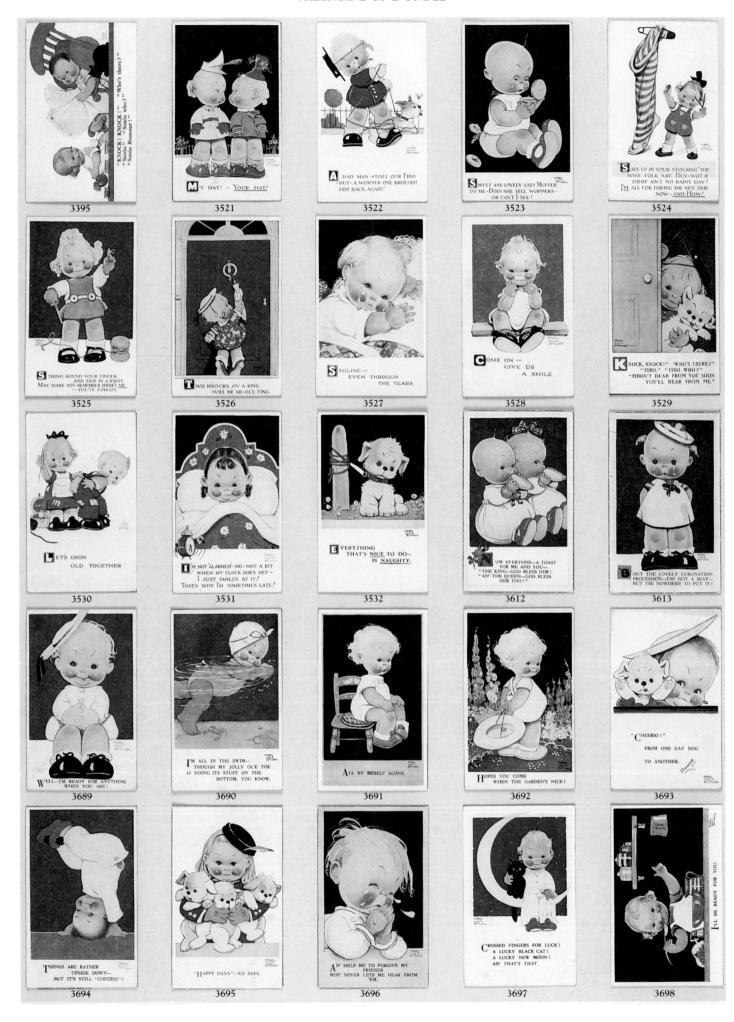

3395

3521

3522

3523

3524

3525

3526

3527

3528

3529

3530

3531

3532

3612

3613

3689

3690

3691

3692

3693

3694

3695

3696

3697

3698

"IT'S 'BLOW EVERYTHING'"
I SAY.

3699

LIFE'S GRAND—
FOR THIS BABY.

3700

I'D LIKE TO SEE MORE OF YOU.

3701

PHYSICAL JERKS—PHYSICAL JERKS
TRY 'EM OL'E DARLIN'
AN' SEE HOW THEY WORKS.
Faites comme moi, vous verrez comme c'est gai.

3702

WOT'S THIS "STORK" ABOUT?

3703

YOU'RE A DEAR OL'E ASS—
I LIKES YOU.

3787

KISS THE PLACE AND MAKE IT WELL.

3788

MARRIAGE—OLE CHAP—IT'S NOT A WORD—IT'S A SENTENCE!

3789

AN' YOU DON'T EVEN WRITE TO ME
NOW. IF I WASN'T A PERFECT LADY
THERE'D BE AN "ORFUL" ROW!

3790

I'SE VERY WELL TREATED HERE.

3791

LET WHO WILL ROAM—I—LIKE ME HOME!

3792

JUS' LONGING TO SEE YOU!

3852

UP TO MY NECK IN THINGS!

3853

LIFE ISN'T REALLY HALF BAD YOU KNOW
IF IT WASN'T THIS ALWAYS "NEEDING"
DOUGH!

3854

LET'S SEE—ANYTHING THE MATTER
WITH YOUR "WRITE" HAND?

3855

REAL SWEET — SAME AS YOU!

3856

ARE YOU ONE OF THE
NAUGHTY ONES?

3857

I'D SHARE MY LAST CRUST WIF YOU!

3858

I'SE THANKING MY LUCKY OLE STAR
THINGS AIN'T NO "WUSSER" THAN WOT
THEY ARE.

3859

FOR YOU!

3860

LET ME BE YOUR GUARDIAN ANGEL.

3861

KEEP ON KEEPING ON—
WHATEVER YOU DO IT IS SURE
TO BE WRONG.

3862

AN' PLEASE FORGIVE
POOR LITTLE WILLY
FOR SAYING HIS PRAYERS IN BED—
IT'S CHILLY.

3863

IT WOULD BE NICE TO SEE MORE OF EACH OTHER!

4178

NO GOOD—BEING GOOD!

4179

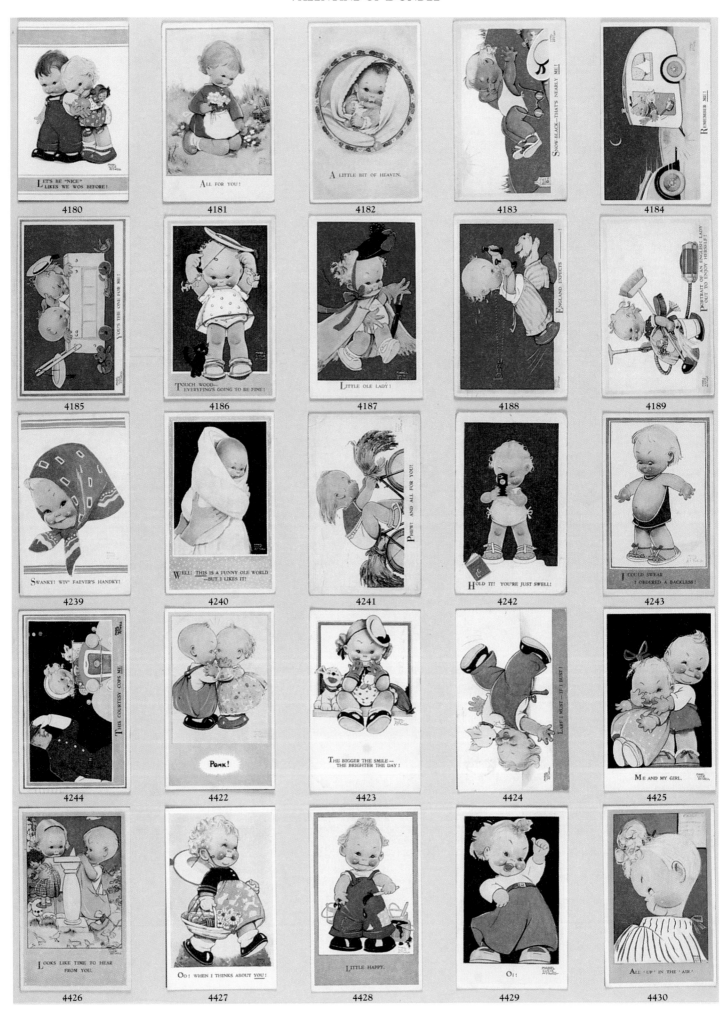

LET'S BE "NICE" LIKES WE WOS BEFORE!
4180

ALL FOR YOU!
4181

A LITTLE BIT OF HEAVEN.
4182

SNOW-BLACK—THATS NEARLY ME!
4183

REMEMBER ME!
4184

YOU'RE THE ONE FOR ME!
4185

TOUCH WOOD— EVERYFING'S GOING TO BE FINE!
4186

LITTLE OLE LADY!
4187

ENGLAND EXPECTS
4188

PORTRAIT OF AN ENGLISH LADY OUT TO ENJOY HERSELF!
4189

SWANKY! WIV' FAEVER'S HANDKY!
4239

WELL! THIS IS A FUNNY OLE WORLD —BUT I LIKES IT!
4240

PHEW! AND ALL FOR YOU!
4241

HOLD IT! YOU'RE JUST SWELL!
4242

I COULD SWEAR I ORDERED A BACKLESS!
4243

THIS COURTESY COPS ME.
4244

PONK!
4422

THE BIGGER THE SMILE— THE BRIGHTER THE DAY!
4423

LARF! I MUST—IF I BUST!
4424

ME AND MY GIRL.
4425

LOOKS LIKE TIME TO HEAR FROM YOU.
4426

OO! WHEN I THINKS ABOUT YOU!
4427

LITTLE HAPPY.
4428

OI!
4429

ALL 'UP' IN THE 'AIR'
4430

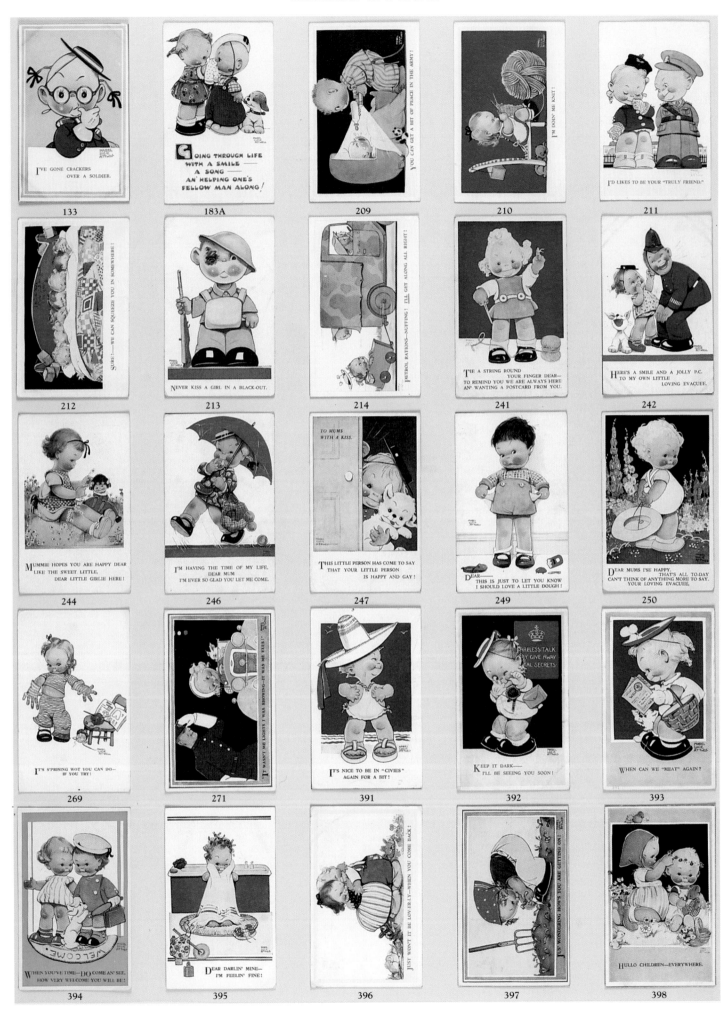

133

183A

209

210

211

212

213

214

241

242

244

246

247

249

250

269

271

391

392

393

394

395

396

397

398

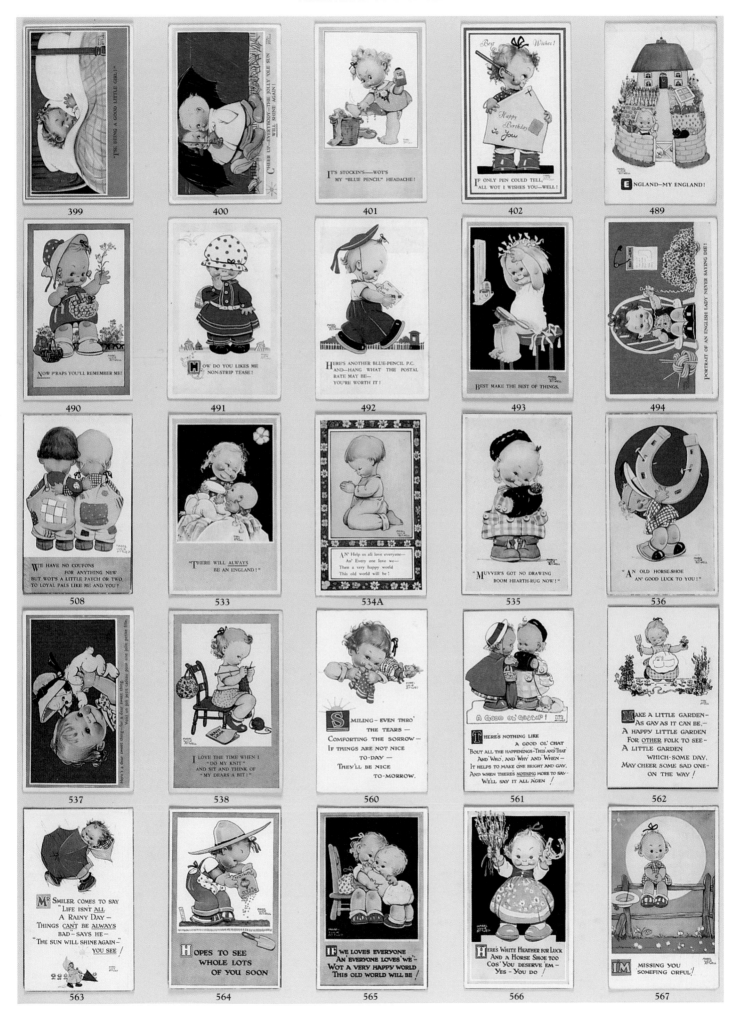

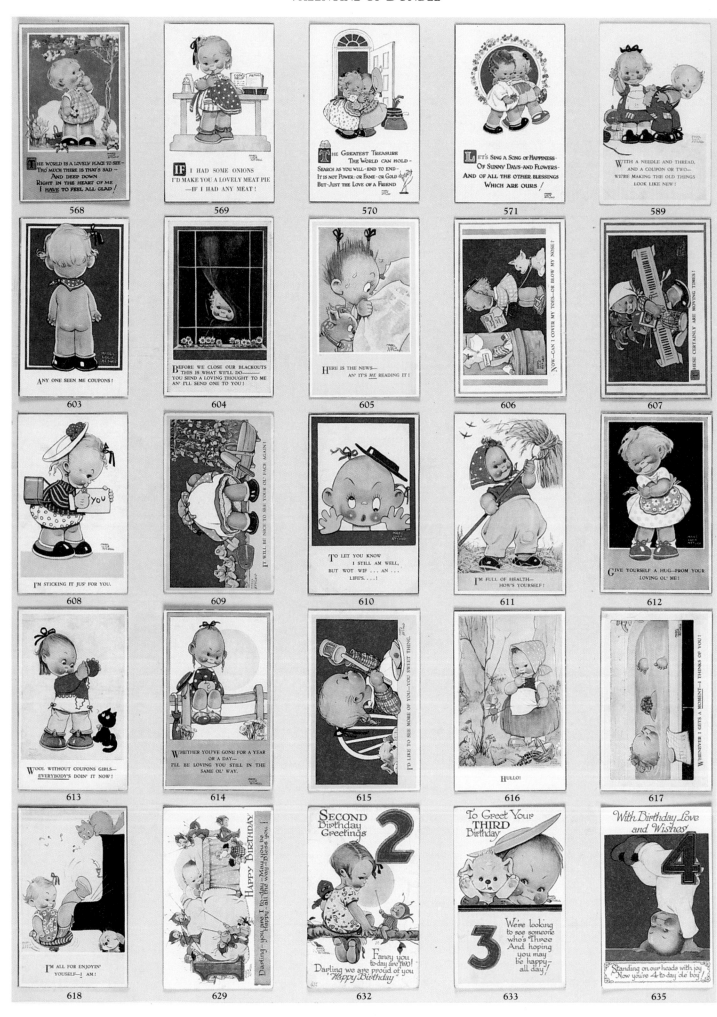

568

THE WORLD IS A LOVELY PLACE TO SEE—
THO' MUCH THERE IS THAT'S SAD—
AND DEEP DOWN
RIGHT IN THE HEART OF ME
I HAVE TO FEEL ALL GLAD!

569

IF I HAD SOME ONIONS
I'D MAKE YOU A LOVELY MEAT PIE
—IF I HAD ANY MEAT!

570

THE GREATEST TREASURE
THE WORLD CAN HOLD—
SEARCH AS YOU WILL—END TO END—
IT IS NOT POWER—OR FAME—OR GOLD
BUT—JUST THE LOVE OF A FRIEND

571

LET'S SING A SONG OF HAPPINESS·
OF SUNNY DAYS·AND·FLOWERS·
AND OF ALL THE OTHER BLESSINGS
WHICH ARE OURS!

589

WITH A NEEDLE AND THREAD,
AND A COUPON OR TWO—
WE'RE MAKING THE OLD THINGS
LOOK LIKE NEW!

603

ANY ONE SEEN ME COUPONS!

604

BEFORE WE CLOSE OUR BLACKOUTS
THIS IS WHAT WE'LL DO—
YOU SEND A LOVING THOUGHT TO ME
AN' I'LL SEND ONE TO YOU!

605

HERE IS THE NEWS—
AN' IT'S ME READING IT!

606

NOW—CAN I COVER MY TOES—OR BLOW MY NOSE?

607

THESE CERTAINLY ARE MOVING TIMES!

608

I'M STICKING IT JUS' FOR YOU.

609

IT'LL BE NICE TO SEE YOUR OL' FACE AGAIN!

610

TO LET YOU KNOW
I STILL AM WELL,
BUT WOT WIF . . . AN . . .
LIFE'S . . . . !

611

I'M FULL OF HEALTH—
HOW'S YOURSELF!

612

GIVE YOURSELF A HUG—FROM YOUR
LOVING OL' ME!

613

WOOL WITHOUT COUPONS GIRLS—
EVERYBODY'S DOIN' IT NOW!

614

WHETHER YOU'VE GONE FOR A YEAR
OR A DAY—
I'LL BE LOVING YOU STILL IN THE
SAME OL' WAY.

615

I'D LIKE TO SEE MORE OF YOU—YOU SWEET THING!

616

HULLO!

617

WHENEVER I GETS A MOMENT—I THINKS OF YOU!

618

I'M ALL FOR ENJOYIN'
YOUSELF—I AM!

629

Happy Birthday
Darling you see I to-day—May you be
Happy—all the way—Bless you!

632

SECOND
Birthday
Greetings 2
Fancy you
to-day are TWO!
Darling we are proud of you
Happy Birthday

633

To Greet Your
THIRD
Birthday
3
We're looking
to see someone
who's Three
And hoping
you may
be happy
all day!

635

With Birthday Love
and Wishes
4
Standing on our heads with joy
Now you're 4 to-day ole boy!

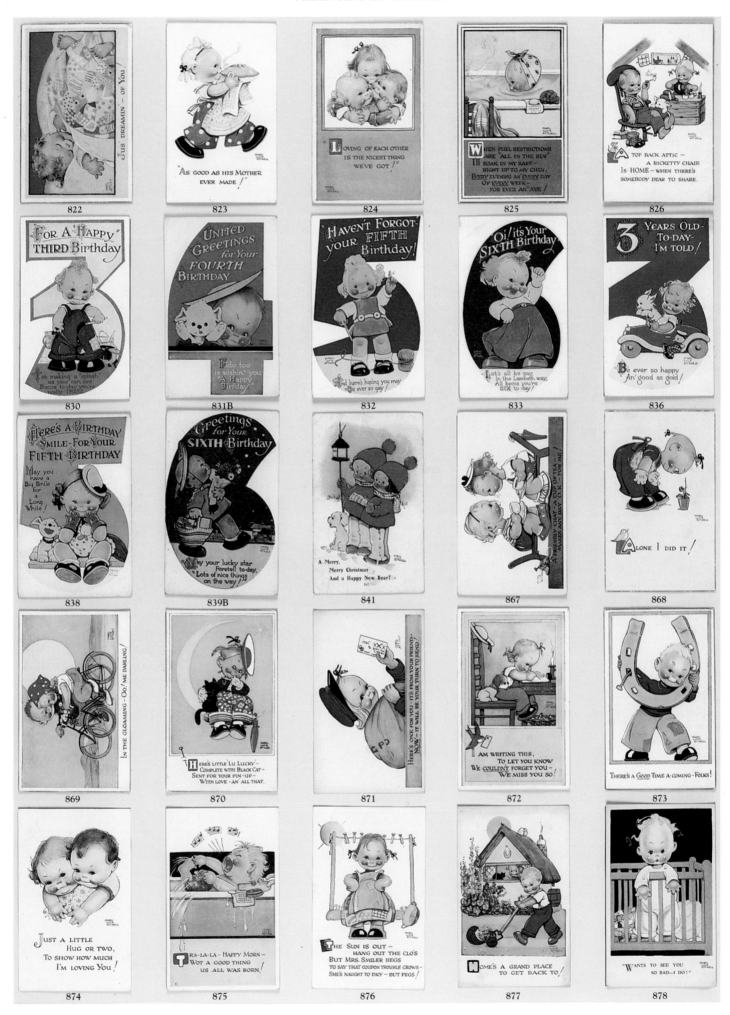

822

823

824

825

826

830

831B

832

833

836

838

839B

841

867

868

869

870

871

872

873

874

875

876

877

878

879

880

881

882

883

884

885

886

887

992

993

994

995

996

997

998

999

1000

1001

1002

1003

1159

1160

1161

1162

1163   Now – what shall us do next?

1164   As I can't give you what I want – I'm sending it!

1165   Why be 'out'-an' on the go' there's something to be said you know for Pussy Cats – an' knitting!

1166   A portrait of two ladies enjoying the peace!

1167   May a Fairy Ring of Happiness surround you – all the way!

1168   Cheerio! Best roll our sleeves up for a real good year.

1169   "This little pig went to Market"

1170   FRIENDSHIP The nicest thing about this life it always seems to me – is while so much costs – Oh! So much the loveliest thing is Free!

1311   To our gardeners Happy, peaceful gardens with flowers of every hue, Making life's way beautiful – We owe them all to you!

1312   String on the finger to help you remember – Don't be forgetting that date!

1313   "Nobody knows the trouble I'm in"

1314   Flowers for the little ones – everywhere"

1315   Fed up!

1316   Another lucky pin-up girl!

1317   God bless all you dears – where ever you be – an' keep you all happy – an' nice – for me!

1318   Happy Chappie!

1319   If there's nothing to 'larf' about – 'larf' at that!

1320   "The sweetest flower that grows"

1321   Sorry I can't come, old dear!

1322   If I didn't 'loves' everybody – I'd 'hates' everybody!

1323   Not snooping – only looking!

1402   May have a new look – but – I'll still be me!

1403   This'll keep 'em quiet – for a bit!

1411   'Spects heaven's a very smart place

1412   How dear of God to make the flowers – to plant them all about He must have loved the firstest day the primroses came out!

1539

1540

1541

1542

1543

1544

1545

1546

1547

1548

1549

1658

1659

1660

1661

1662

1663

1664

1665

1666

1667

1668

1669

1670

1771

"FANCY PANTS!"
1772

THE FRIEND OF MAN.
1773

I'D SHARE MY LAST CRUST WITH YOU—BUT I'VE EATEN IT!
1774

CAN'T MAKE ENDS MEET— SO I'M GETTING COLD FEET.
1784

THE NICEST THING ABOUT GOING AWAY IS TO GET BACK HOME AGAIN.
1785

LITTLE SISTER— NEW FROM HEAVEN.
1786

BETTER MAKE A CHANGE— IF A CHANGE MAKES YOU BETTER.
1787

HOWEVER MUCH IT COSTS YOU— IT'S YOUR DUTY TO LOOK YOUR BEST.
1788

I'M PUTTING YOU ON MY LIST OF DEARS.
1822

JUST A BUNDLE OF LOVE.
1853

MUST FEED 'EM!
1861

ALL THE WORLD IS FULL OF GLADNESS— EVERYWHERE!
1862

SHE DOES THE JOBS ABOUT THE HOUSE— SHE WASHES UP WITHOUT A GROUSE— SHE GIVES THE FURNITURE A RUB AN'—WOT IS MORE— SHE COOKS THE GRUB!
1863

"I'D GIVE YOU MY ALL" HE SAID WITH A SIGH— "BUT A FELLOW MUST LIVE" SHE SAID "BUT WHY!"
1864

DOWN IN THE FOREST SOMETHING STIRRED!
1865

A WEE CHAMPION.
1866

HAVE YOU EVER HEARD THE FLUTTER OF WINGS— THE HURRYING BY OF FEET AND THINGS? PERHAPS WHAT YOU HEARD WAS ONLY A BIRD— I WONDER—I WONDER—I DO!
1868

"GOOD MORNIN" FROM ONE CHEERY SOUL TO ANOTHER!
5049

WITH LOTS OF LOVE AND KISSES!
5050

HIS MASTER'S WEE BIT LASSIE!
5051

STILL ON THE SAME OL' JOB!
5052

DON'T OVERDO YOURSELF— DARLING!
5053

I TIDY MY THINGS— ALL NICE—AWAY— BUT—I NEVER REMEMBERS WHERE!
5054

CHEERIO— IT MAY NEVER HAPPEN!
5055

I'M ALWAYS THINKING 'BOUT YOU!
5056

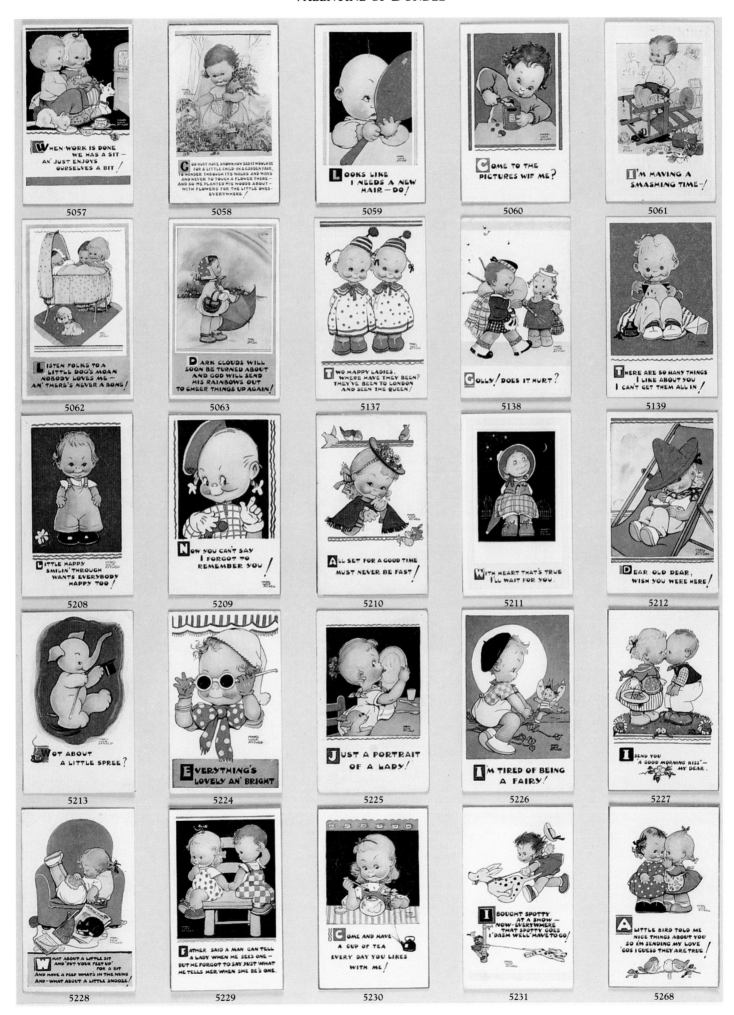

5057

5058

5059

5060

5061

5062

5063

5137

5138

5139

5208

5209

5210

5211

5212

5213

5224

5225

5226

5227

5228

5229

5230

5231

5268

A woman's duty.

IF YOU CAN'T BE CAREFUL BE GOOD.

YOU COULDN'T KNOW I'D MISS YOU SO!

THIS ONE'S FOR YOU, DEAR.

Carlton   Valentine 2471   Valentine 3108   Valentine 660

Books published by W. & R. Chambers, 1905-1914.

In 1902, Raphael Tuck & Sons was the first publishing house to employ Mabel Lucie Attwell. These early books were designed in England and printed in Germany before the First World War.

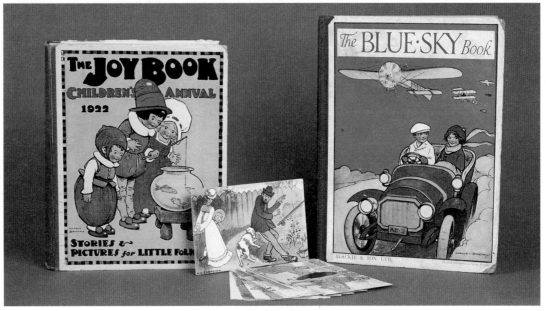

Harold Earnshaw, Mabel Lucie's husband, was a commercial artist. He produced postcard designs, and also illustrated many books for boys during the 1920s, including these covers for annuals for E. Hulton & Co. Ltd.

BOOKS

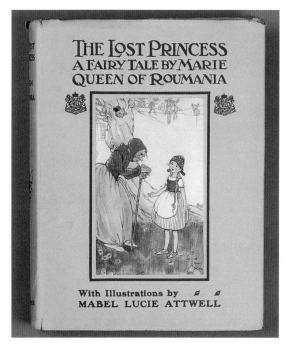

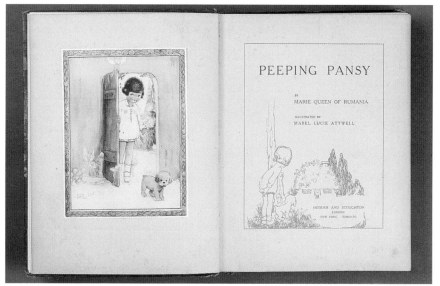

Mabel Lucie collaborated with Queen Marie of Romania to produce these books. Left: *The Lost Princess*, S.W. Partridge & Co., 1924; above, *Peeping Pansy*, Hodder & Stoughton, 1919.

The earliest Mabel Lucie Attwell books designed for Valentine of Dundee were these attractive shaped-books in a series of nine. Six were fully illustrated with 'interesting reading matter', the remaining three were painting books.
NB the reverse of the cut-out book illustrates the range, c1910. *The Lucie Attwell Rocker Book* far right, 1930s.

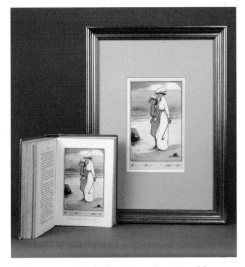

Above, original drawing for *Troublesome Topsy and Her Friends*, W. & R. Chambers, 1913.

Above right, *The Raphael Tuck Library of Gift Books* comprised thirty-one volumes, all edited by Capt. Edric Vredenburg with six books illustrated by Mabel Lucie. Each volume came in a box decorated with an identical illustration to the book cover, 1910-1917.

Right, *The Boo-Boos Series* by Valentine & Sons, 1920-1922. Mabel Lucie's *Boo-Boos* were charming, chubby-faced pixies dressed in Lincoln Green. They featured for the first time in *Bunty and the Boo-Boos* and later the diminutive 'do-gooders' appeared on postcards, plates and prints.

Page from *The Long Ago Postcard Painting Book*, Raphael Tuck & Sons.

Comforting Thoughts, written and illustrated by Mabel Lucie Attwell, Valentine, c1940.

Four blue books published by W. & R. Chambers, 1905-1911.

BOOKS

Mabel Lucie Attwell illustrations for the *All About …* books, published by John Swain, 1925.

The first Mabel Lucie Attwell annual, top left, was published by S.W. Partridge & Co., in 1922 and annuals continued to be produced for fifty-two years. The early annuals were all undated, the first to be given a year of publication was the 1959 edition published by Dean & Son. The last annual, bottom right, was published in 1974.

One of a series of posters for the London Underground which brought Mabel Lucie Attwell to the attention of the wider public, c1905.

Mabel Lucie Attwell's earliest poster work in the first decade of the twentieth century was for The Dumb Friends' League in London, a charity which held an annual 'Country Fair' to raise money for the care of sick animals. The 1910 poster advertised the Coronation Fete as well as the Fair. Mabel Lucie's style was influenced by John Hassall, President of the London Sketch Club.

ORIGINAL ARTWORK

Mabel Lucie Attwell
stored most of her
original artwork on the
assumption that she
might be able to re-use a
popular subject in
another context. Top
left, *Troublesome Topsy
and Her Friends*, 1913;
top centre, *This One's
For You, Alright!* a
postcard design (2030),
1931; remaining
pictures, the *Boo-Boos*
series, 1920-22.

ADVERTISEMENTS

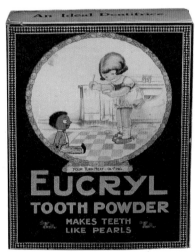

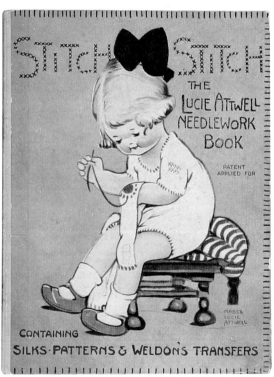

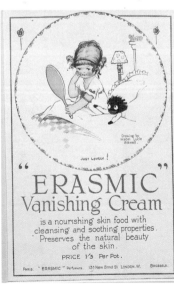

Following the success of her postcard designs for Valentine of Dundee, advertisers used Mabel Lucie Attwell designs for their various products. Her chubby children were soon extolling the virtues of bedtime drinks, baby foods, vanishing creams, tooth powder, fountain pens and knitting patterns.

JIGSAWS

Right, unusual book with hankies and an uncut jigsaw, c.1950.

Victory, c1950.

Victory, c1950.

Maker unknown, c1935.

Tower Press, c1960.

Victory, c1950.

Left and above, puzzle and box, A.V. Jones & Son, c1920.

This bathroom plaque was the most popular item designed by Mabel Lucie, selling in its millions worldwide. Since its introduction by Valentine of Dundee in 1927, several versions have been produced and lines added to the original verse. Mabel Lucie also created a brand new verse which read: *'To you who occupy this place, A little hint or two in case, You linger longer in the water, Than a person really oughter, Reading perhaps of pash or crime, 'Til it's long past dinner time! 'Sides there's sure to be a queue, Waiting to come after you!'*

CALENDARS AND PLAQUES

Calendars and plaques for all occasions. Mabel Lucie's meaningful verses were to be found in every room of the house.

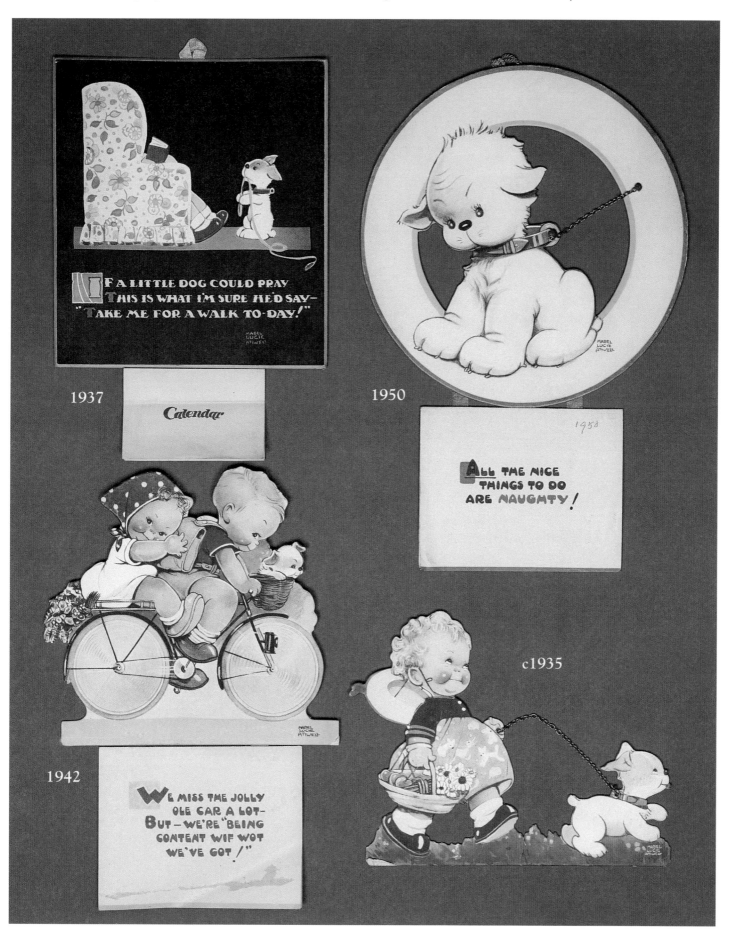

1937

1950

1942

c1935

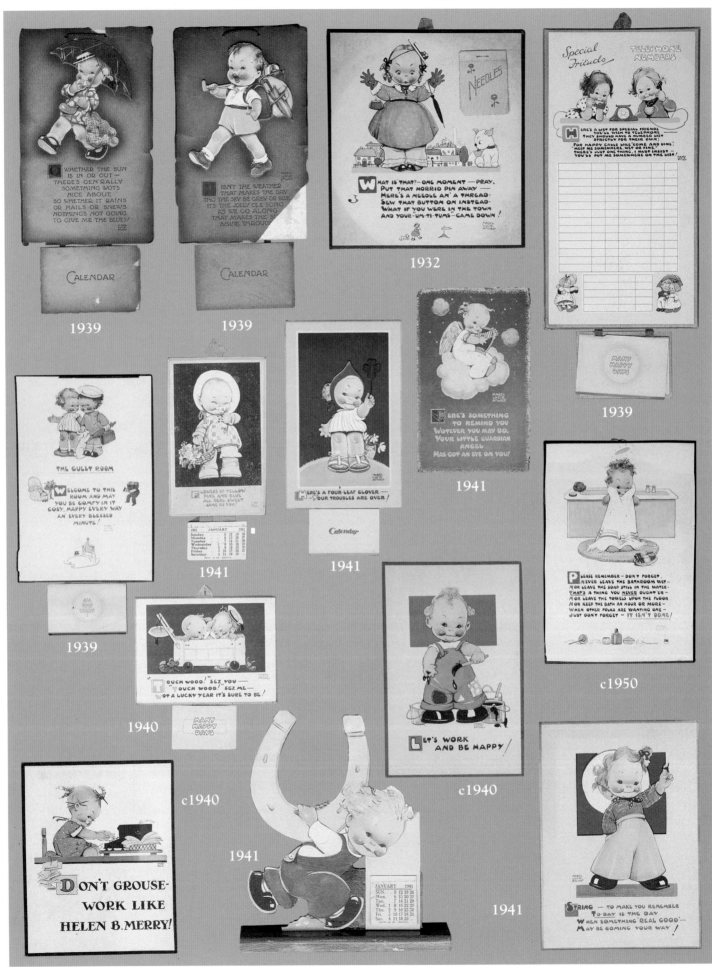

1932

1939

1939

1939

1941

1939

1941

1941

1941

c1950

1940

c1940

c1940

1941

1941

1939

1938

1940

1940

1940

1940

c1950

1939

1942

c1928

1942

1941

c1935

c1935

1940

1936

c1940

1940

1931

c1930

1952

1932

1938

1938

1937

1933

1934

1933

1932

MABEL LUCIE ATTWELL DESIGNS FOR SHELLEY CHINA

Shelley Potteries Ltd., (formerly Wileman & Co.) of Foley China Works, Longton, Staffordshire, introduced their first Mabel Lucie Attwell designs for children in 1926. Most of their tea ware was made in bone china and their baby plates in earthenware. The success of Mabel Lucie Attwell is evident by the number of her designs and the associated publicity and advertising. The figure series was introduced in 1936 and, after the wartime restrictions were lifted, a limited amount of tableware was reissued. The following illustrations of nursery ware show the majority of shapes and designs (for further shapes, including the elusive napkin ring, see *Gifts for Good Children Part II* p157, by Maureen Batkin).

Mabel Lucie Attwell Designs for Shelley China

For *Donkeys and Carts* see letter from Shelley China to Mabel Lucie, page 27.

NB The all-earthenware hot-water dish for keeping food warm.

From left, *Golfer* LA8, *I's Goin' Tata* LA18, *Our Pets* LA19, *I's Shy* LA9, *Toddler* LA1, from the original series of nine, introduced in 1937. For *Diddlums* and *How'm I doin?*, see publicity leaflet on page 99.

MABEL LUCIE ATTWELL DESIGNS FOR SHELLEY CHINA

Nursery ware, the jampot lacks its lid.

Baby plates, including a hot-water dish with metal underside.

From left: foreign porcelain figure after the postcard *And You're Another So There!*; nursery ware; one of the original seven *Boo-Boos*; the orange squeezer introduced in 1936; and a post-war mug, Solian Ware by Simpsons Ltd., Cobridge, c1950.

MABEL LUCIE ATTWELL DESIGNS FOR SHELLEY CHINA

Chamber pots, right, boy's version, Woods Ivory Ware.

Tea service with Regent teapot, c1950.

Bridegroom LA6 and bride LA5.

Boo-Boo condiment set and Sleepy Head nightlight, introduced 1936.

Modelled mushroom teaset with Boo-Boo milk jug, 1926.

Jug replacing Boo-Boo modelled jug, and covered jug, introduced 1937.

98

MABEL LUCIE ATTWELL DESIGNS FOR SHELLEY CHINA

Boo-Boos, the mermaid, the mushroom village and a figure of a boy, probably introduced post-war. (Photograph courtesy of the authors of *Shelley Potteries*, 1980.)

Chicken, duck and rabbit animal-teaset, introduced 1930.

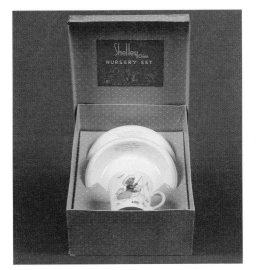

Boxed nursery set, c1950.

Above, six of the seven original modelled *Boo-Boos*, introduced in 1937.

Pages from publicity leaflets.

Alternative colourway for 'Precocious Kids'. *I's Shy* LA9, *Toddler* LA1, introduced in 1937.

Parchment lamp shades.

Money-box biscuit tins for Crawford & Sons.

Printing set, No.529, maker unknown.

Cut-out figures in cardboard by Valentine were an addition to the company's giftware range in the 1920s. The cricketer with his duck on a lead, amused the sports-minded and the couple cannoodling on a gate have romantic appeal. The girl even wears a real red ribbon.

Birthday cards by Valentine.

Valentine party place-cards.

Sanderson cut-out motifs.

Small metal-framed plaques with verses mostly written by Mabel Lucie Attwell proved popular for Valentine of Dundee after the Second World War.

Mabel Lucie Attwell and George Studdy paper picnic ware for Valentine.

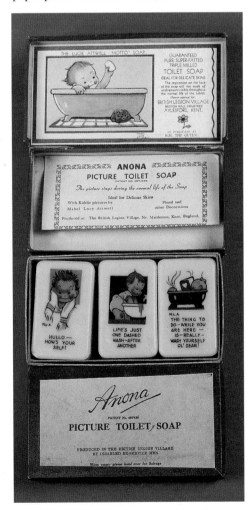

Building bricks with pictures on all six faces. Pre First World War, made in Germany.

'Dundee' picnic ware plate, Valentine; Lucie Attwell kiddies' cutlery, maker unknown.

Designs on tablets of soap made in the British Legion Village nr Maidstone, Kent. This raised funds for the Legion after the Second World War.

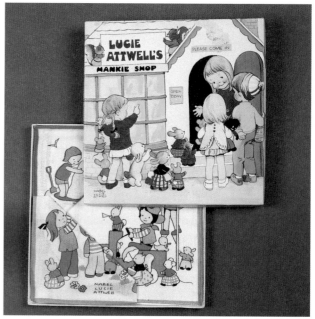

Mabel Lucie's designs for kiddies' hankies showing nursery rhymes, royal occasions and the inevitable *Boo-Boos*. Mostly produced after the Second World War.

DOLLS

Above: left, Germanic doll, *Hygenic* with blond plaits, Chad Valley; right, *Mabel Lucie 5100* doll, Chad Valley.

Right, *Bambina* dolls, a series of soft dolls with jointed velveteen limbs and painted features, Chad Valley, 1932.

Diddums dolls, first modelled by Mabel Lucie in plasticine. A plaster cast was then created, mass produced in rubber (above) and celluloid by the Cascelloid Co., 1930s.

ENESCO

In 1987, using original Mabel Lucie Attwell designs, the Chicago-based Enesco Corporation created a range of ceramic figurines. Several hundred of these have been produced and a Collectors' Society in the U.S.A. boasts a 20,000 strong membership.

Above from left to right: *Look Out, Something Good Is Coming Your Way; You Won't Catch Me Being A Golf Widow; Friendship Has No Boundaries; The Future – God Bless 'Em; A Little Help from Fairyland.*

Left, pages from the Enesco catalogue, 1997.

PEGGY WICKHAM

Towards the end of her life Mabel Lucie encouraged her daughter to continue designing books and product design in her mother's style.

MEMORIES OF MABEL LUCIE

As my collection of all things 'Mabel' grew and grew, the journalist in me wanted to know more about this charismatic woman who created the cards, calendars and cheeky characters that were so much a part of my childhood. Who was she? Where did she live? Was she part of a team or an incredibly industrious individual? What was the secret of her continuing popularity and had success made her rich and, perhaps, remote? In search of more information, I was fortunate to be able to interview some of those who knew her.

Oil painting of Peggy Wickham, only daughter of Mabel Lucie, by her son, Mark Wickham. She was in her late sixties when she sat for this last portrait.

PEGGY WICKHAM, DAUGHTER

I knew that Mabel had died on the 5th November 1964 in Fowey, Cornwall, and discovered that her children, Peggy and Peter, were living at the 'Old Rectory', an impressive seventeenth-century house in Froxfield near Marlborough in Wiltshire. After a somewhat prolonged correspondence, we arranged to meet and, on the 29th October 1976, I set out from Brighton on the three-hour journey to Froxfield. Peggy was clearly not in the best of health. Her brother, Peter, pottered about in the background keeping one ear

on our conversation as he helped to prepare an informal lunch which we shared around the kitchen table. It was a cold day and the tape-recorded interview (later to be heard on B.B.C's *Woman's Hour*) took place in front of an open fire which snapped and crackled disconcertingly. Peggy patiently answered my questions – which she must have been asked many times before – with a gentle air of resignation. Did she recognise herself in any of her mother's illustrations? She replied:

'I find that a very hard question to answer. I don't think so. I know that some of the books were dedicated to us.'

What of the fashions of the time, big bows and short skirts?

'I can just recognise the bows from my early childhood because most of my friends were wearing them but, in fact, I think I never wore one myself because I was dressed in a rather modern way for the time, with bobbed hair and sweaters.'

I asked whether Peggy's childhood had been a happy one. After all, she described her mother as 'always working'. Her answer was emphatic:

'It was a very, very happy childhood. My mother was very good to us and very protective I'm sure and perhaps a bit spoiling, but we were free to run in the fields, and wild flowers were everywhere then. It was excellent, just right. This was a new outlook about children; I think her friends and her generation were paying much more attention to their children and, if you like, spoiling them much more than their parents did.'

Was this reflected in her mother's work?

'She seemed to be very original... one of the first people to use children as symbols for grown-ups with titles suitable for grown-ups and to express things that grown-ups were feeling through these children.'

I suggested to Peggy that Mabel Lucie Attwell had been a forward-thinking person in many ways and had, for example, some interesting views about postcard production.

'Yes, she was always saying "I like white on white" and one hadn't realised at the time that it was really a rather revolutionary idea. But this is one of the appeals of her work I think, the way she places very delicate colours against a white background. And, of course, she was always trying to get publishers, particularly in the later days, to appreciate this because they would say, "No – we must have coloured backgrounds – white backgrounds get dirty in the shops." She always disliked that.'

In the late 1950s, towards the end of her mother's career, Peggy took over responsibility for producing *Mabel Lucie Attwell* postcards, annuals and other work. When I showed Peggy some of her own cards from my collection she was dismissive and told me they weren't worth keeping. 'Oh you don't want to collect those', she chided. I gained the impression that she had been somewhat reluctant to take on the task of maintaining her mother's extraordinary output, knowing that she was an almost impossible act to follow. Peggy's final annual for Dean & Son under the *Lucie Attwell* banner was published in 1974.

As I got ready to leave the Old Rectory, I asked Peggy whether her mother would have been pleased by the renewed interest and enthusiasm for her work:

> 'I'm very, very sorry that she's missed it. She began to have a little of it before she died. A young man came down and interviewed her for *Vogue*. I think he meant to come and make fun of her but, in fact, it turned out to be a very nice interview indeed. And I said, after this, "Hello – you're having a real comeback aren't you?" and she enjoyed that. ...I only wish she could see more of this going on now.'

Just before I left, Peggy spoke to me 'off the record'. She was unwell and concerned that because of this there might be no-one to organise a celebration of her mother's forthcoming centenary. She asked if anything could be done? I was happy to reassure her and on the 4th December 1979, the Mabel Lucie Attwell Centenary Exhibition opened in the Brighton Museum. Peter Earnshaw and other members of the family were there but, sadly, Peggy was not. She had died on the 30th November 1978.

Sketch of her brother Peter, by Peggy Wickham.

Mabel Lucie's son, Peter Earnshaw, at the doorway of his former home in Rye, Sussex, 1992.

PETER EARNSHAW, SON

In the last years of her life, Mabel Lucie Attwell lived with Peter in Fowey. He acted as her secretary and ran errands. Peter was a sociable man who was well-liked by the local people. He spent many evenings in local pubs, his favourite being The Lugger where, refreshed by a Guinness or two, he would play the piano. His nephews, Mark and John Wickham, recall summer holidays when their 'nice Uncle Peter' would take them to the pub and play 'his jazz'. They also remember him as a good cook and a keen joke-teller.

I first met Peter at Froxfield in 1976 when he chose to stay very much in the background while I spent much of the afternoon talking with his sister, Peggy. He seemed reluctant to discuss his mother with anyone, particularly a journalist. Contrary to Peggy's view that Mabel Lucie would have been delighted with the renewed interest in her work, Peter insisted that this would not have been the case. 'She wouldn't have wanted the publicity,' he argued. Three years later at the Centenary Exhibition in Brighton he was more forthcoming and spoke to me at length as we toured the exhibits.

I asked him what it was like having a well-known mother:

'When you're brought up as a kid, you don't take any notice of the fact that your mother is a famous artist. You take it for granted. That's how it's always been.'

Had Mabel Lucie used her children as models? He confirmed Peggy's view:

'No, I don't think so – except she may have got a general idea – things we got up to and so on.'

What about his own artistic ability and was he ever asked to help his mother in her studio? Peter chuckled:

'Certainly not. I can't even draw a straight line... There was one occasion, a plain straightforward picture of a car... all you saw was the radiator and the front mudguards – very carefully traced from somewhere or other. I ruled it all out and did everything mathematically.'

He confirmed that his mother kept all her illustrations:

'A lot of it was wanted over and over again by the publishers... so everything was kept in apple pie order in a filing cabinet.'

As far as I could tell, Peter never had what could be described as a 'proper job'. He was an enigmatic man who enjoyed his own company on long, solitary walks through the countryside of Sussex and Cornwall and yet was equally at home playing the piano in crowded public bars, surrounded by friends and strangers alike. Peter and I kept in touch after the exhibition. He lived alone in Brighton for a while and then moved to Lewes in East Sussex. He continued with his piano playing but developed what was thought to be Alzheimer's disease. In 1991 he moved into a residential home but in the summer of 1992 he went missing and was found dead from natural causes the following day, by a police helicopter.

The Sussex Express when reporting his death, described him as a 'bit of a loner and a wanderer'. No reference was made to his mother and I think that is the way Peter would have liked it. I can hear his gruff voice insisting, 'She wouldn't have wanted the publicity, and neither would I.'

JOHN AND MARK WICKHAM, GRANDSONS

For school children enjoying summer holidays on the south coast of Cornwall, the area around the picturesque town of Fowey has to be paradise. John and Mark Wickham would spend several weeks during the summer in St. Fimbarrus Road with their grandmother and Uncle Peter. I met them at John's house, a short drive from the centre of Northampton, and Mark recalled those 'idyllic' holidays:

'Peggy used to drive us down from Froxfield in an Austin 10...with a dinghy and canoe on the roof. One of the strongest memories of that journey was the point where we would wake up in the morning and see those white mountains of china clay as we came across Bodmin Moor... The combination of my grandmother being a very hard-working, serious person who provided this lovely place to go to, and Uncle Pete being the amusing chap who kept us entertained. I mean, at that age it was

John Wickham, sitting beneath a sketch of himself asleep as a boy, drawn by his mother, Peggy.

very romantic. Life on the water in boats and meeting young people at the sailing club... It was a tremendously exciting place to be.'

John remembered his grandmother as always working and, like Peter before them, the boys were occasionally allowed to help by drawing the front end of a motor car. Mark explained:

'Cars were a big part of her life because she was always the owner of grand cars. She encouraged us to have them. Even gave us one each, at one point. She was famous before our time. She had already decided in Fowey to take less of a part in public life – she'd made a decision to go down there... and just quietly get on with her work.'

Mabel Lucie regularly visited the family home in Froxfield in the 1950s and even sat for Mark when he was developing his skills as a portrait artist.

'She was a very good sitter, she sat by one of the windows and it was just a natural thing for me to do at that stage.'

He recalled a happy moment when his grandmother suddenly pulled up the hem of her long skirt and said, 'Not bad for an old 'un!' But, he added, she could be quite stern too:

Mark Wickham with his oil painting of his grandmother, Mabel Lucie. The nine-foot tall easel (Reeves & Son, London) can also be seen in the early photograph of Mabel Lucie taken at her home in Coulsdon, Surrey (see page 13).

'I remember when a young friend and I got rather out of hand at Froxfield... doing all sorts of naughty things. She came downstairs with her chin trembling – she always trembled when she got angry – and she said, "I'm not going to be party to this." '

Today, through the offices of Lucie Attwell Ltd., both John and Mark share the responsibility for keeping their grandmother's work alive. At his home in Devizes, Mark retains her original easel and gives pride of place to his portrait of the woman who, despite her stern countenance, brought so much pleasure to a couple of teenage schoolboys on their summer holidays in Cornwall.

The late Michael Wickham, father of John and Mark, 1993.

MICHAEL WICKHAM, SON-IN-LAW

On the 13th November 1929, under a photograph of Mabel Lucie Attwell's only daughter, the *Daily Sketch* announced the engagement of 'Miss Peggy Earnshaw... to Mr Michael Wickham...' They were married the next summer at Chelsea Registry Office but, according to Michael, it was a 'terrible mistake'.

We met in 1993 when he was living just outside Swindon. A fine-boned man with a shock of white hair, Michael made me very welcome and offered warm bread from the oven, local cheese and a glass of home-brewed beer. Mick (as he was known) and Peggy met as students at the Royal Academy Schools in London:

'She was six months younger than me. We were far too young... I should never have married her... I tried to get out of it but you can't imagine the pressures that were brought on you by middle-class families at that time. You just can't break up something... I'm glad I didn't because the results' (his sons) 'haven't been entirely bad!'

I asked him about his mother-in-law:

'She was a darling. I admired her very much. She was formidable... I was frightened of her at first. She had this schoolmistress quality. Full of rectitude... but sensible, nice rectitude. She was a good person... She was a great success. She was single-minded about it which was lovely really, and defended it all costs. But perfectly prepared to laugh when we teased her about it, when we recited *Don't Forget – Never Leave the Bathroom Wet*, that sort of thing. We used to chant it. She always liked that. She was an extremely tenacious woman but the thing I remember most about Mabel Lucie was that she was an extraordinarily nervous person. She was anxious about the world all the time. She had absolutely no sort of scientific grasp about physical reality so she thought every conceivable thing was potentially dangerous even when it wasn't...'

Peggy had told Michael that when she was young, Mabel Lucie used to tie cushions over the projections from pieces of furniture, so that the children 'wouldn't bump their little heads'.

I was sad to hear of Mick's death in 1994.

BERYL DELVE, COMMUNITY NURSE

In the early 1960s Beryl Delve left her native Liverpool to become a community nurse in Fowey, little realising that she would be coming into contact with two of the town's most famous residents – Daphne du Maurier and Mabel Lucie Attwell. This, as she explained to me when we met, presented certain difficulties when on her rounds as to which of the two VIPs should she visit first:

'I felt General Browning (du Maurier's husband), should be visited in the morning and Mabel Lucie was quite happy to have me in the afternoon so long as I would stay to have afternoon tea with her. Tea was served on a tray with very nice china by Peter. She'd have been lost without him. She was mostly confined to bed. I think her main trouble was her fragility. When she smiled and got to know you a bit, and opened up you realised what a wonderful lady she was.'

The two women got on well and talked a great deal. Beryl remembers Mabel Lucie Attwell's interest in current affairs:

'She read the papers very well... Not just one, I think she took several and compared... she talked to me about the news and I was expected to make comments.'

Sadly, Beryl was away from Fowey when Mabel Lucie died. She has affectionate memories of her famous patient and particularly remember her eyes:

'It was all in her eyes. Twinkling there. Oh, full of life, yes!'

The Mabel Lucie Attwell Museum in Fowey.

BOOKS WRITTEN AND ILLUSTRATED BY MABEL LUCIE ATTWELL

That Little Limb, May Baldwin,
    W&R Chambers, 1905
Troublesome Ursula, Mabel Quiller-Couch,
    W&R Chambers, 1905
The Amateur Cook, K. Burrill & Anne M. Booth,
    W&R Chambers, 1906
Dora, A High School Girl, May Baldwin,
    W&R Chambers, 1906
All About A Little Dog, (cut-out book),
    Raphael Tuck & Sons 1907
Busy Bees & Play Hours, 'Father Tuck's Indestructible Board Series',
    Raphael Tuck & Sons 1908
A Boy And A Secret, Raymond Jacberns,
    W&R Chambers, 1908
The Little Tin Soldier, Graham Mar,
    W&R Chambers, 1909
The February Boys, Mrs Molesworth,
    W&R Chambers, 1909
Old Rhymes,
    Raphael Tuck & Sons, 1909
The Old Pincushion, Mrs Molesworth,
    W&R Chambers, 1910
That Troublesome Dog, Raymond Jacberns,
    W&R Chambers, 1910
Grimm's Fairy Tales,
    Cassell & Co., 1910
Fairy Tales, Stories and Legends,
    Cassell & Co., 1910
My Dolly's House, ABC,
    Raphael Tuck & Sons, 1910
Mother Goose,
    Raphael Tuck & Sons, 1910
Alice in Wonderland, Lewis Carroll,
    Raphael Tuck & Sons, 1911
Tabitha Smallways Schoolgirl, Raymond Jacberns,
    W&R Chambers, 1911
Grimm's Fairy Stories,
    Raphael Tuck & Sons, 1912
Little Lucie,
    Valentine & Sons, 1913
Troublesome Topsy and Her Friends, May Baldwin,
    W&R Chambers, 1913
Our Playtime Picture Book,
    Raphael Tuck & Sons, 1913
A Band of Mirth, L.T. Meade,
    W&R Chambers, 1914
Hans Andersen's Fairy Tales, ed. Capt. Edric Vredenburg,
    Raphael Tuck & Sons, 1914
Hans Andersen's Fairy Stories, ed. Capt. Edric Vredenburg,
    Raphael Tuck & Sons, 1915
The Water Babies, (abridged version) Charles Kingsley,
    Raphael Tuck & Sons, 1915
Children's Stories from French Fairy Tales, Doris Ashley,
    Raphael Tuck & Sons, 1917
Fairy Tales, Stories & Legends, Hans Andersen,
    Cassell & Co.
Peeping Pansy, Marie, Queen of Romania,
    Hodder & Stoughton, 1919
Wooden, Archibald Marshall,
    Collins, 1920
Fairyland,
    Thomas Nelson & Sons, 1918

Puss in Boots and other Fairy Tales,
    Thomas Nelson & Sons, 1920
Youngest Reader's Fairy Tales,
    Thomas Nelson & Sons
Peggy - The Lucie Attwell Cut-Out Dressing Doll,
    Valentine & Sons, 1921
Peter Pan and Wendy, J.M. Barrie,
    Hodder & Stoughton, 1921
The Boo-Boos Series:
    Bunty and the Boo-Boos
    The Boo-Boos and Bunty's Baby
    The Boo-Boos at School
    The Boo-Boos at the Seaside
    The Boo-Boos at Honeysweet Farm
    The Boo-Boos and Santa Claus
    Valentine & Sons, 1920-22
Baby's Book,
    Raphael Tuck & Sons, 1922
Stitch Stitch – The Lucie Attwell Needlework Book,
    Valentine & Sons, 1922
Lucie Attwell's Bedtime Stories,
    S.W. Partridge & Co., 1923
Lucie Attwell's Merry Time Stories,
    S.W. Partridge & Co., 1923
Lucie Attwell's Tea Time Stories,
    S.W. Partridge & Co., 1923
Mother Goose – Nursery Rhymes for Baby,
    S.W. Partridge & Co.
Lucie Attwell's Tales for Bedtime,
    S.W. Partridge & Co.
Lucie Attwell's Tales for Teatime,
    S.W. Partridge & Co., 1924
Lucie Attwell's Tales for All Times.
    S.W. Partridge & Co., 1924
The Lucie Attwell Picture Books,
    S.W. Partridge & Co., 1924-1928
The Lost Princess, A Fairy Tale, Marie, Queen of Romania,
    S.W. Partridge & Co., 1924
Lucie Attwell's Twilight Tales, M.L. Attwell & A.G. Herbertson,
    S.W. Partridge & Co., 1925
Lucie Attwell's Firelight Tales,
    S.W. Partridge & Co., 1925
Lucie Attwell's Going to Bed Tales,
    S.W. Partridge & Co., 1925
All About Bad Babies,
    John Swain, c1925
All About the Seaside,
    John Swain, c1925
All About Fairies,
    John Swain, c1925
All About the Country,
    John Swain, c1925
All About School,
    John Swain, c1925
All About Fido,
    John Swain, c1925
Lucie Attwell's Bedtime Tales,
    S.W. Partridge & Co., 1926
Lucie Attwell's Merry Time Tales,
    S.W. Partridge & Co., 1926
Lucie Attwell's Tea Time Tales,
    S.W. Partridge & Co., 1926

Le Rêve de Lulu,
    Librarie Hachette, Paris, 1927
Lucie Attwell's Cuddle Time Tales,
    S.W. Partridge & Co., 1927
Lucie Attwell's Kiddie Winks' Tales,
    S.W. Partridge & Co., 1927
Lucie Attwell's Wide Awake Tales,
    S.W. Partridge & Co., 1927
Lucie Attwell's Tuck Away Tales,
    S.W. Partridge & Co., 1928
Allerlei Von 'Fido',
    Vienna Wolf, 1928
Young Peggy in Toyland, Archibald Marshall,
    Collins, 1928
The Golden Goose:
    Little Red Riding Hood
    The Little Brother and Sister and Other Stories, Brothers Grimm
    The Tinder Box
    Thumbelina and Other Stories, Hans Christian Andersen
    Raphael Tuck & Sons, 1929
Peter Pan and Wendy, retold by Mary Byron (2vols),
    Hodder and Stoughton, 1929
Lucie Attwell's Cheerie Tales,
    S.W. Partridge & Co., 1929
Lucie Attwell's Chick-a-bid Tales,
    S.W. Partridge & Co., 1929
Lucie Attwell's Cutie Tales,
    S.W. Partridge & Co., 1929
The Red Shoes and Other Stories, Hans Christian Andersen,
    Raphael Tuck and Sons, 1930
The Wild Swans, Hans Christian Andersen,
    Raphael Tuck & Sons,
Lucie Attwell's Rock-Away Tales, (various authors),
    S.W. Partridge & Co., 1930
On the Way to Fairyland, Grace Floyd,
    Raphael Tuck & Sons
Lucie Attwell's Rainy Day Tales, (various authors),
    S.W. Partridge & Co., 1931
The Little Shepherdess, Hans Christian Andersen,
    Raphael Tuck & Sons, 1932
Lucie Attwell's Fairy Book,
    S.W. Partridge & Co., 1932
Lucie Attwell's Happy Day Tales,
    S.W. Partridge & Co., 1932
Lucie Attwell's Quiet Time Tales,
    S.W. Partridge & Co., 1932
Lucie Attwell's Twilight Tales,
    S.W. Partridge & Co., 1932
Lucie Attwell's Big Midget Book,
    Dean & Son, 1934
Lucie Attwell's Painting Books,
    Dean & Son, 1934
Lucie Attwell's Great Big Midget Book,
    Dean & Son, 1935
Lucie Attwell's Playtime Pictures,
    Carlton Publishing Co., 1935
Comforting Thoughts, M.L. Attwell,
    Valentine & Sons, c1940
For Today 'Golden Thoughts' booklet,
    Valentine & Sons, c.1940
Lucie Attwell's Story Book,
    Dean & Son, 1943
Lucie Attwell's Story Book,
    Dean & Son, 1945
Lucie Attwell's Book of Stories,
    Dean & Son (undated)
Lucie Attwell's Story Book
    Dean & Son, 1950

Lots of Things,
    Birn Bros., c1950
'Manty' A Fairy Tale,
    Birn Bros., c1950
Lucie Attwell's Jolly Book,
    Dean & Son, 1953
Lucie Attwell's Story Book,
    Dean & Son, 1953
Lucie Attwell's Pop-Up Book,
    Dean & Son, 1956
Lucie Attwell's Nursery Rhymes Pop-Up Book,
    Dean & Son, 1958
Lucie Attwell's Storytime Tales,
    Dean & Son, 1959
Dean's 'Little Poppet' Series:
    A Little Bird Told Me
    A Little Bird Told Me Another Story
    Little Poppet ABC Book
    Story for a Poppet
    The Giant's Boot
    Dean & Son, 1959
Lucie Attwell's ABC Pop-Up Book,
    Dean & Son, 1960
Lucie Attwell's Book of Verse,
    Dean & Son, 1960
Lucie Attwell's Rocker Book,
    Dean & Son, c1960
Lucie Attwell's 'Happy Times' Pop-Up Book,
    Dean & Son, 1961
Lucie Attwell's Painting Book,
    Dean & Son, 1961
Lucie Attwell's Book of Rhymes,
    Dean & Son, 1962
Lucie Attwell's Humpty Dumpty Rhymes Pop-Up Book,
    Dean & Son, 1963
Lucie Attwell's Painting Book, No.2,
    Dean & Son, 1963
Lucie Attwell's Stories for Every Day (various authors),
    Dean & Son, 1964
Lucie Attwell's Tinies' Book of Prayers,
    Dean & Son, 1967
Lucie Attwell's Tiny Rhymes Pop-Up Book
    Dean & Son, 1967
Lucie Attwell's Painting Book, No.4
    Dean & Son, 1967
Lucie Attwell's Tell Me a Story Pop-Up Book,
    Dean & Son, 1968
Lucie Attwell's Book of Rhymes
    Dean & Son, 1969
Lucie Attwell's Super Book of Fun,
    Dean & Son, 1969
Lucie Attwell's Bumper Book of Fun,
    Dean & Son, 1973
The Water Babies, Charles Kingsley,
    Piccolo, Pan Books Ltd, 1973
Grimms Fairy Tales,
    Piccolo, Pan Books Ltd, 1974
Lucie Attwell's Goodnight Stories, ed. produced exclusively for
    W.H.Smith, Deans International Publishing, 1984

MABEL LUCIE ATTWELL ANNUALS
The Lucie Attwell Annual Nos 1, 2 & 3,
    S.W. Partridge & Co., 1922, 1923, 1924
Lucie Attwell's Children's Book,
    S.W. Partridge & Co., 1925-1932
Lucie Attwell's Annual,
    Dean & Son 1934-1974

DESCRIPTIONS OF THE COVERS OF UNDATED ANNUALS 1922-1958

Based on original research by Bill Lofts.

1922 Toddler girl in sleeping suit holding a puppy whilst sitting on half moon in sky.

1923 Girl with puppy under each arm.

1924 Little girl in green frock, holding green basket in which a pixie is riding. Another five pixies are walking alongside.

1925 Girl with dog, sitting on bough of tree – at the end of the branch is a nest holding two fairies.

1926 Girl on donkey with puppy and doll also riding.

1927 Boy and girl riding on the back of a large white duck.

1928 Toddler riding in a donkey cart at night.

1929 About twenty small characters including tin soldier and large yellow duck in blue bonnet.

1930 Three long panels with strips of characters: i)characters, ii)toddler wheeling baby, iii)car full of characters held up by policeman.

1931 Boy and girl riding in cart pulled by donkey with two pigs in back.

1932 Little girl thumping on large black piano.

1933 No annual published. (NB British Library has a second copy of the 1932 annual stamped August 1933.)

1934 A very large full face of toddler with caption 'Hallo, Here we are again'.

1935 Toddler holding umbrella and bag of apples, with a puppy on a lead.

1936 Child and big bunch of flowers with *Boo-Boo* at feet.

1937 Toddler holding a big bunch of flowers, marching along in large black shoes.

1938 Boy and girl with puppy looking out of window.

1939 Girl holding up a puppy that is wearing a yellow bonnet with a black ribbon.

1940 Boy (holding flower) and girl astride a donkey with puppy.

1941 Boy riding trike with red wheels with girl on the back, holding cat.

1942 Three girls, one lamb, numerous birds, bright red background. First story: *Jo and the Boo-Boos.*

1943 Girl holding lamb. First story: *Bunty has a job of work.*

1944 Boy and girl with puppy in green boat fishing close to an occupied lighthouse.

1945 Girl wearing a yellow frock looking up at a tree where two birds are in a nest. Two rabbits sitting below.

1946 Boy and girl in circle surrounded by pets/animals etc. including a large duck and small white elephant.

1947 Girl wearing blue overalls and a very large hat, spraying flowers with green watering can.

1948 Boy and girl at door welcoming pets that include small pixies, a duck and a teddy bear.

1949 Girl and boy with numerous pets, including a giraffe in a green basket balloon in the sky.

1950 Boy holding puppy in midst of flowers. Small elf looking on.

1951 Boy looking through telescope with two girls rolling a giant snowball with the help of some friends.

1952 Boy and girl with friends on boat named *Adventure.*

1953 Boy and girl at open window with puppy. Seated on the sill are two pixies, a mouse and a robin.

1954 Girl in *Red Riding Hood* dress holding a bunch of holly and a doll. Boy holding mistletoe and half-eaten biscuit.

1955 Boy and girl, in their arms a white cat, golly and a teddy.

1956 Two boys and two girls playing *Ring-a-Roses* with golly and teddy.

1957 Girl with large bonnet holding up very large flowers. Four elves holding onto them.

1958 Boy in blue-white striped jersey picking cherries from tree.

1959 - 1974 Annuals are dated.

BOOKS, ANNUALS AND PERIODICALS CONTAINING SOME ILLUSTRATIONS BY MABEL LUCIE ATTWELL

Father Tuck's 'My Dolls House ABC',
Raphael Tuck & Sons, c1905-1907

Father Tuck's Nursery Series 'Twice One are Two ABC',
Raphael Tuck & Sons, c1905-1907

Father Tuck's Fairyland Picture Book,
Raphael Tuck & Sons, c1905-1907

Mother Goose Postcard Painting Book,
Raphael Tuck & Sons

The Long Ago Postcard Painting Book,
Raphael Tuck & Sons

The Diary of a Baby,
Eveleigh Nash, London, 1907

Playbox Annual 1910,
The Amalgamated Press Ltd., 1910

Valentine's Dolly Books:
    Jack's The Boy
    Little Bright Eyes
    Little So-Shy
    Me and Fido
    Our Babs' Nursery Rhymes ABC
    Sister Susie and the Twins
    Tommy Tucker
    Valentine & Sons, 1913

Valentine's Painting Books:
    Ever So Nice Painting Book
    Isn't it Good Painting Book
    Just the Thing Painting Book
    Valentine & Sons, 1913

From Nursery Land, 'Father Tuck's Life Like Series',
Raphael Tuck & Sons, 1915

Playtime Pages, 'Father Tuck's Welcome Gift Series',
Raphael Tuck & Sons, 1915

The Golden Hours Library (12 vols, 8 by Mabel Lucie Attwell)
Raphael Tuck & Sons

Princess Marie-Jose's Children's Book,
Cassell & Co. Ltd., 1916

Nursery Tales,
Thomas Nelson & Sons Ltd., 1924

Robin Redbreast Story Book,
Blackie & Son Ltd., 1925

A Bunch of Cousins (dust jacket), L.T. Meade,
W&R Chambers Ltd.

Uncle Sam's Money-Box (cover), Mrs S.C. Hall,
W&R Chambers Ltd.

The Buttercup Story Book (frontispiece),
Blackie & Son Ltd.

The Daffodil Story Book (frontispiece),
Blackie & Son Ltd.

The Queen's Book of the Red Cross,
Hodder & Stoughton, 1939

Tiny Tots, (front cover 1914),
Cassell & Co. Ltd., 1920

Little Folks,
Cassell & Co. Ltd., numerous

Father Tuck's Annual,
Raphael Tuck & Sons

Father Tuck's Golden Gift Series,
Raphael Tuck & Sons

Strand Magazine, numerous

Pearson Magazine, numerous

NOVELTY CARDS

Although these cards have an individual number shown on the front of the card, all the designs have been used previously and their original Valentine card numbers are shown in parenthesis. Some of the very early designs were not numbered.

1059 (un-numbered)	1573 (1395)	1748 (881)	1831 (3528)	1916 (879)
1069 (un-numbered)	1624 (1963)	1749 (2739)	1832 (3103)	1918 (751)
1073 (un-numbered)	1628 (1988)	1750 (2648)	1834 (3700)	1919 (536)
1242 (un-numbered)	1629 (1813)	1755 (2642)	1836 (3695)	1920 (3701)
1366 (4704)	1632 (1897)	1771 (2923)	1837 (3690)	1927 (132)
1370 (4813)	1633 (1811)	1774 (2918)	1838 (3529)	1931 (871)
1371 (un-numbered)	1673 (2030)	1775 (2925)	1859 (4183)	1933 (391)
1372 (un-numbered)	1695 (2407)	1776 (2919)	1860 (3792)	1965 (1432)
1374 (un-numbered)	1700 (2419)	1790 (2833)	1861 (3787)	1966 (1434)
1376 (4704)	1709 (1803)	1791 (2888)	1862 (4242)	1967 (1438)
1377 (4313)	1721 (1354)	1795 (2915)	1863 (3791)	5647 (5647)
1539 (1339)	1728 (2474)	1798 (2916)	1885 (4423)	Australian card –
1543 (1338)	1736 (2645)	1813 (2887)	1886 (4424)	*Greetings from*
1572 (1350)	1741 (2418)	1830 (3702)	1908 (2406)	*Streaky Bay*

BIRTHDAY CARDS

Although some birthday cards show an individual number, the majority of designs had been used previously and were given a separate series or set number or letter. Several cards were given the same set or series letter in the early years and where this applies the original card numbers are listed. In later years, where both a letter and number appear on a card, the original design number is in parenthesis. Valentine & Sons also produced a series of 'Golden Scroll' relation birthday postcards.

1925	**1927**	K1 (1761)	N5 (2044)	A/6 (508)	Set No2
Series B	**Set E**	K3 (1590)	N6 (2138)		3523
976	1242	K4 (1591)	N7 (2188)	B/2 (2647)	3526
979	1247	K7 (1592)	N8 (2190)	B/3 (2645)	3529
1000	1248	K8 (1764)	N11 (2039)	B/4 (2561)	3532
1002		K9 (1707)	N12 (2561)		
1008	**1928-1929**	K11 (1584)	O2 (1990)	C/1 (2831)	**Set No3**
1010	**Set F**	K12 (1585)	O7 (2040)	C/3 (2923)	3859
	1271		O9 (2126)	C/5 (2920)	4181
*Series 1112X	1285	L1 (1815)	O12 (2142)	C/6 (2887)	4242
1008	1305	L2 (1813)			
1013	1597	L5 (1957)	P1 (2309)	D/1 (2921)	**Set No4**
1014		L6 (1806)	P2 (2315)	D/3 (2922)	4186
1015	**Set G**	L7 (1962)	P3 (2305)	D/4 (2919)	4241
	1341	L8 (1804)	P5 (2405)	D/6 (2829)	
1926	1342	L9 (1806)			**Set No5**
Series C	1343	L10 (1802)	Q1 (2306)	F/1 (2737)	4591
1011	1551	L11 (1895)	Q2 (2310)	F/2 (3022)	4753
1092		L12 (1807)	Q3 (2313)	F/3 (2469)	
1097	**Set H**		Q4 (2314)	F/4 (3025)	**Set No6**
1099	1398	M1 (1894)	Q5 (2411)	F/5 (3026)	398
1171	1399	M3 (1811)		F/6 (1958)	
1172		M4 (1890)	R1 (2418)		**Set No7**
1173	**1929-1931**	M5 (1958)	R2 (2417)	G/2 (3285)	393
1174	E1 (1354)	M7 (1988)	R3 (2422)	G/3 (3281)	402B
Set D	E3 (2030)	M8 (1959)		G/6 (3098)	493
1178	E4 (1594)	M10 (1892)	S3 (660)		535
1180	E5 (2914)	M11 (1893)	S4 (2475)	H/1 (3279)	537
1183	H3 (2041)	M12 (1812)	S5 (1549)	H/2 (3103)	538
1185	J3 (1594)		S6 (2308)	H/4 (3105)	
1187	J6 (1703)	**1932-1934**		H/6 (3109)	**Set No8**
	J10 (2142)	N2 (2187)	**1934-1936**		394
	J11 (1706)	N4 (2135)	A/1 (2136)	**1936-1942**	565
			A/3 (2641)	**Set No1**	566
			A/4 (2739)	3531	568

The following cards were reprinted as birthday cards during the Second World War, but were not given any identifying letter or number: 241, 2303, 4423, 4433. ***Series 1112X** above, are Christmas cards.

VALENTINE & SONS POSTCARDS 1954-1963

The following postcards are not illustrated as most of these were the work of Mabel Lucie's daughter, Peggy Wickham.

1954

5316	Too Busy To Write!
5317	Good Night Sleep Tight - Another Nice Day Tomorrow!
5318	Says One 'Trusty Friend' To Another, Come On - Let's Have A Word From You!
5319	Must Have A Little Sob-Stuff Sometimes!
5320	Away With Troubles And Darksome Doubt! Best Have A Fairy Or Two About!
5321	There Is A Little Town With Streets All Up-All Down, Where Happy Folk Will Meet And Dance Along The Street!
5322	"It's Equal Rights - It's Equal Pay - They Haven't No Time For Me Today!" Says Cupid
5323	I Say My Prayers So I Can Get All Good - But They Hav'n't Been Answered Yet!
5324	Sing A Song Of Rainy Days, We Cannot Do Without 'Em, It's Rain Helps The Flowers Grow - Rain Fills The Pools An' Ponds Just So Ducks Can Swim About 'Em!
5325	Lucky White Heather It's All For You - It Didn't Cost Nothing So I'm Lucky - Too!
5326	It's Better To Laugh Than Cry - By-Far So - Altogether Now - Ha-Ha-Ha!
5327	Here's Love To Those Who Cook Our Eats - And Think Up Things For Special Treats
5328	Over To You!
5329	"They'll Know What I've Done For Art - When I'm Dead!" "Well You'll Be Safe Out Of The Way Miss" He Said!
5330	How Good Of God To Make Us All!
5331	"Why Use A Saucer And A Cup" Says Us - Wot Does The Washing Up!

1955

5354	Well! Some Prefer A 'Girlie' Girl!
5355	Never Say 'Dye'!
5356	Another New Day To Be Glad In - Busy, Good, Gay - Or Be Bad In!
5357	Now I Shall Know If You Loves Me!
5358	White Heather For Luck An' All For You, Becos' You, Deserve It 'Deed You Do!
5359	When God Made The World And The Birds All To Sing, The Tommys, The Janes And The Marys, The Flowers, Sky And Grass And Each Lovely Small Thing, He Just Had To Put In Some Fairies!
5360	Is It The Hats Wot's Wrong - Or Me?
5361	I'm Being Contented With My Lot!
5362	Each New Morning This Is What We'll Do - You Send A Loving Thought To Me An' I'll Send One To You!
5363	I Shot My Arrow Into The Air. How The … Was I To Know Old Grumpy Bones Was There?
5364	Simply Must Have A New Frock For The Hols!
5365	If You Do Get A Job Done There's Sure To Be Another Wants Doing!
5366	Now We've Been An' Gone An' Done It!
5367	What A Lovely, Lovely World God's Made - For You And Me!
5368	I'm Asking For A Blessing Becos' I'm Sure You Know, It's Us Awful Naughty Ones Need Blessings So!
5369	Never A Trouble Never A Care - Just Bobbing About Any Ol' Where!
5370	V.I.P.

1956

5492	Meet Me At The Corner!
5493	I Go To Church On Sunday All Good An' Sweet An' Fair - I Go To Church On Sunday 'Cos I likes The 'Hims' Wot's There!
5494	Two Young Robins Chirpy And Bright, Both In Agreement That Life's All Right!

5495	Wot Are The Wild Waves Saying!!
5496	Must Be 'All Nice' For When You Come!
5497	Don't Stay Away Too Long!
5498	"Meet 'Kinkie' - One Of God's Chillun"
5499	Them Mermaids!
5500	Hoping To See Something More Of You Soon!
5501	I'm Asking For A Blessing, Because I'm Sure You Know, It's Us Awful Naughty Ones Need Blessing So!
5502	Shall Us? Lets!
5503	The True Friend Will Always Know When To Come And When To Go!
5504	Don't Wake Me Up, I'm Dreaming Of You!
5505	Just Bringing You A Few Flowers!
5506	Hello, You Dear!
5507	A Garden Is A Blessed Place - Some Blessed Thing To Do In It - Every Blessed Day!
5508	If We Love Everyone An' Everyone Loves Us, This Will Be A Happy World An' Save A Lot Of Fuss!
5509	Missing You Something Awful!
5552	This Economy Squeeze May Be A Good Wheeze, But We Must Have Some Flowers!

1957

5640	Bless Me! Don't Count Your Worries - Count Your Blessings - Bless You!
5641	Anyway - It Don't Snore!
5642	He Says He Wants More Money!
5643	If It's Not One Darned Thing - It's Another!
5644	With My Washing Machine, From Morning Till Night, I Wash Every Blessed Dashed Rag Within Sight!
5645	If Things Don't Go On As We Hoped - S'pose We Can Still Go On Hoping?
5646	"God's Flower - For Eager Baby Hands"
5647	I Have My Eye On You!
5648	Couldn't You Loves Me - Whiskers - Or No Whiskers?
5649	"Hope You Come When My Garden's Nice!"
5650	'Nuf Said!
5651	I Say - You Don't Say!
5652	My Hat!
5653	Peace - Heavenly Peace!
5654	We Can't All Come Out Of The 'Top Drawer' But We Can Have A Lovely Bottom Drawer!
5655	Keep On Smiling!
5656	I'll Soon Learn 'Em I'm Around!
5657	With Love - From Me

1958

5754	Happy Heart - Happy Day!
5755	Any Chance Of You Hoving In Sight?
5756	It's The Girl In His Heart Wot Makes A Man Sing - Plunking All Day On His Plunkity Thing
5757	Best Love Your 'Love' With A Cookery Book!
5758	I'm Just Keeping My Head Above Water - How're You Doing?
5759	Here - There - Or Any Ol' Where!
5760	Almost As Good As Mum Makes!
5761	A Horse Shoe Brings Luck We've Heard That Before So I Send The Whole Horse An' That Gives You Four!
5762	Hopes You'll Be A'Looking Out For Us!
5763	An' Make 'Em See He Never Means To Be The Awful Dog He Seems!
5764	Everyone's Round The Bend - Dear!

1959

5828	*Why Look At T.V. When You've Got Me?*
5829	*From Loving Me To Lovable You!*
5830	*I'd Better Be Nice And Smart For You!*
5831	*If I Didn't Loves You - I'd Hates You!*
5832	*I'm Expecting You - Darling!*
5833	*It Takes All Sorts To Make A World And I'm Glad You're One Of The Sorts!*
5834	*Happy Days!*
5835	*I'm Always Dreaming Of Getting A Bit Of Peace - But!*
5836	*Oh - Yes We Have A Washing Machine - But - Who Does The 'Blessed' Ironing - Me!*
5837	*What Would They All Do Without Us?*
5838	*Out Of The Everywhere Into Here - An' Loving It!*
5839	*Hark - Hark! A Seat In The Park!*
5840	*Stay As Sweet As You Are!*
5841	*Must Have A Bit Of Leisure - For Pleasure!*
5842	*Lots Of Fish - No Chips!*
5843	*Sunny Days!*
5844	*If You Want To Get Going - You Must Get Going!*
5845	*S'pose I'm Enjoying Myself!*

1960

5918	*Best For A While Try One's Best Smile!*
5919	*I'm Leading A Bit Of A Dog's Life!*
5920	*I'm In The Usual Rush - But I Haven't Forgotten You!*
5921	*Don't Let 'Em Spoil Our Moon!*
5922	*Whistling Along - Heart Full of Song, And You!*
5923	*Busy Days Are Happy Days!*
5924	*I'm Making A Bee-Line For You, Sweet!*
5925	*I Like It Here!*
5926	*Everything's A-Growing - Everything's Gay!*
5927	*Come On Darling, Let's Get Going!*
5928	*Looks A Nice Old World To Me!*
5929	*Getting Away From It All*
5930	*See You Soon!*
5931	*Things Aren't So Bad!*
5932	*All "Flower Happy" - Makes Me Think Of You*
5933	*Hopes This Finds You As It Leaves Me At Present*
5934	*Guess Who I'm Thinking Of?*
5935	*Everything's Just Fine Here!*
5936	*Could You Love Me For Myself Alone?*
5937	*I'm Alright Jack!*
5938	*Far From The Kitchen Sink*
5939	*It's Work-Work-Work!*
5940	*I'm S'posed To Be Cooking The Dinner!*
5941	*Now I've Time For A Nice Think About You!*

1961

6020	*You'll Know Where To Find Me!*
6021	*What's Cooking Now?*
6022	*Hope You'll Get All Bright And Gay Now You've Heard From Me Today!*
6023	*It's Never Too Late To Mend - Or - To Write To Your Dear Old Friend!*
6024	*Everything That's Nice To Do - Is Naughty!*
6025	*Thought You Might Like To Hear From Me!*
6026	*I'm Out To Enjoy Life!*
6027	*In A Bit Of A Mix But I Know Who I Like!*
6028	*It's Lovely Just To Have A Sit And Think Of All Of You A Bit!*
6029	*If Ever I'm Through - I'll Be Seeing You!*
6030	*Nicer Than Mink I Think - More Cuddly!*
6031	*We're All Right - How's Yourself?*
6032	*You've Got Me All Of A Whirl!*
6033	*Life Would Be Fine If You'd Send Me A Line!*
6034	*Look Who's Here!*
6035	*All Right So Far!*
6036	*Just A Little Note To Remind You There's Me!*
6037	*Life's Busy But It's Grand!*
6038	*A Friend For Keeps!*
6039	*Don't Worry I Can't Play The Dashed Thing!*

6040	*You're Nice!*
6041	*I'll Soon Be In The Swim Here!*
6042	*Home Sweet Sweet Home!*
6043	*I Take A Good View Of You!*

1962

6122	*Bright Interval Due, So Perhaps I'll See You!*
6123	*Strikes Me Any Time's Tea-Break Time*
6124	*It's Time I Saw You Again*
6125	*Someone's Happy - If It's Only Me!*
6126	*It's Lovely To Get Right Away - And Fill No Forms In For A Day*
6127	*Life's A Helluva Sweat - But We Won't Say 'Die' Yet!*
6128	*Look Smart - And Keep Your Fingers Crossed!*
6129	*I'll See You Tonight*
6130	*Won't Go Too Far Away, Dear*
6131	*Let Who Will Roam, I Like It At Home*
6132	*We Peep Out And The Sun Peeps In; That's A Grand Way For A Day To Begin*
6133	*A Girl Loves A Sweetie To Keep Her Gay And Glad; You're The Sweetest Sweetie A Girl Ever Had*
6134	*Too Busy To Write But Send This To Show You, There Are Spots Of Peace In This Old World To Go To*
6135	*Am Gradually Getting My Foot In Here, And Soon Will Be All In The Swim, Ol' Dear*
6136	*If The News Is Bad Today, Turn It Off, And Let's Be Gay!*
6137	*The Hats Are So Lovely I Feel That I Must Buy Me Another - Tho' It Makes Me Go Bust*
6138	*This Is A Lovely Town - That Was*
6139	*Jobs To Do Will Never Stop, But I Hope You Are Feeling Right On Top*
6140	*Hope You Come When The Garden's Neat, And Plenty Of Everything Fresh To Eat!*
6141	*Think Of Me When These Flowers You See, And I Shall Be Thinking Of You!*
6142	*I May Not Be Good, But Try As I Should To Be Good Looking - Any Girl Would!*
6143	*Wherever I Am, Whatever I Do, Somehow I Seem To Be Dreaming Of You!*
6144	*Whenever I'm Roaming My Thoughts All Go Homing - To You!*
6145	*Everybody Had Better Watch Out - No-one Shall Bite You While I Am About!*

1963

6224	*You're 'Top Of The Tops'!*
6225	*I'll Be Along Soon!*
6226	*More Chores - But I'll See You Soon!*
6227	*It's Little Things Wot Bring Us Pleasure Hope You Get Yours In Double Measure!*
6228	*Can't All Be The 'Cover Girl' Type!*
6229	*Shall Never Be Ready For Anything But Send You My Love And An X!*
6230	*Hope Everything's Running Smoothly With You!*
6231	*If You Let Yourself Go - Everything Goes!*
6232	*Everything's Fine!*
6233	*With A Little Luck I'll Be Seeing You Soon*
6234	*Can't Wait To See You!*
6235	*A Little Bird Told Me - You'd Like Me To Write!*
6236	*Away From It All But Not Too Far Away!*
6237	*You're In My Heart Wherever You Are!*
6238	*If We Can't Be Rich We Must Be Clever!*
6239	*It Is Nice Here!*
6240	*Let The Weather Be As It May - Nothing Will Stop Me Going Away!*
6241	*Things Go On As They Should, Never Had It So Good!*
6242	*Hi! Ducks - Remember Me?*
6243	*Life's A Tearing Rush But I'm Keeping Cheerful!*
6244	*You Are My Line!*
6245	*Thinks My Lucky Star's About Due!*
6246	*Hope I Strike The Right Note With You!*
6247	*Do Come Along When The Garden's Neat, Flowers All About And Looking A Treat!*

POSTCARDS – TOPICAL SUBJECTS

Mabel Lucie's postcards were characterised by her meaningful, optimistic captions and verse. They were bought in their millions and the illustrations were often indicators of topical subjects such as fashion, social mores and significant events. Cards from 1916 included wartime subjects, *All For The Love Of A Soldier* (4012), and girls with fashionable black bows in their hair, *I Was A Good Little Girl Til I Met You* (4308). 1917 saw more black bows in 'bobbed' hair, and the hopeful, *A Sign Of Peace* (4425). In 1918, *What Next?* (4482) was a sign of changing times – and in 1921 Mabel Lucie introduced her *Boo-Boos*. The growing popularity of crossword puzzles was reflected in many of her 1924 postcards, *Crossword Puzzles* (805) as were crystal sets (809). In came the Charleston in 1926, *I'd Rather Charleston With You* (1176), and the following year saw a subtle change of style with the introduction of smaller figures, *Times Is Awful...* (1241). She created a new character, *Snookums*, in 1928, *If You Want A Boy, There's Always Me* (1303). The general election of 1929 was recorded by such captions as *Wot Ever You Do – I Votes For You* (1545), and Mabel Lucie's love of patchwork and dungarees was evident in 1930, *Cheerio! Good Luck Often Comes In Patches!* (1808), as were her hats in 1931, *You Should Come Here And See The Sights!* (1960). There was a musical theme to many of the 1932 cards and references to unemployment, *An' What Did You Do In The Great Big Slump?* (2314). Increased use of a red background in 1933/4, *What About A Spot Of Fun...* (2423), was followed by the black backgrounds of 1935 (perhaps influenced by her son's death), *Sure – You're Swell!* (3022). In 1938 the 'Lambeth Walk' was a fashionable dance as is seen by *Oi!* (4429). 1939 gives rise to many cards with wartime themes, *Johnny Get Your Gun* (4748), and these continue throughout the war years: camouflage, *Petrol, Rations – Nuffing!...* (214); landgirls, *Just Wondering How's You Are Getting On* (397); food and clothes rationing, *If I Had Some Onions...* (569) and *Wool Without Coupons Girls...* (613); the blackout, *Before We Close Our Blackouts...* (604); the wartime economy, *Oh Yes! – Ours Is A Utility Baby!* (756). Optimism and patriotism are to the fore in 1944/5, *Cheerio! I've Still Got Lots To Be Thankful For!* (811) and *An' Where Do You Think Great Britain Would Be...* (813). In 1945 Mabel Lucie moved to Cornwall and her cards carried cheerful peacetime messages, *There's A Good Time Coming Folks* (873). During 1946/7 the English preoccupation with weather was reflected, *I'm Coming Along – If I Have To Swim For It!* (1160), and in 1949 a rustic theme, *To Our Gardeners* (1311). In 1955 there were the first indications of the collaboration between the artist, now seventy-six years old, and her daughter Peggy and in 1960 Mabel Lucie's last postcard showed a small child standing in the sea, saying *S'pose I'm Enjoying Myself* (5845). Peggy then took over the artwork and her more modern approach was established.

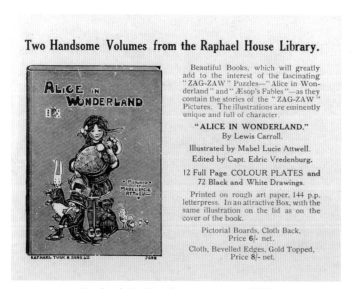

Raphael Tuck's advertisement, c1912.

Order from Mabel Lucie Attwell for artist's materials.